I0098145

THIS IS

GOD'S

WORLD

LISTEN AS HE SPEAKS TO US

1st Peter 3:15

In your hearts set Christ apart as holy [and acknowledge Him] as Lord. Always be ready to give a logical defense To anyone who asks you to account for the hope that Is in you, but do it courteously and respectfully.

DR. ROGER L. HARRELL

AUTHOR

Dr. Roger L. Harrell

Roger Harrell was 26 years away from a doctorate in Educational Administration when he was born in Clovis, New Mexico to Dorothy and Reagan Harrell. He earned that degree from the University of New Mexico in Albuquerque. His life has been very much devoted to teaching in Public Schools and serving as Superintendent of Schools for 18 years. Additionally, he worked one year in the U.S. Office of Education before it was captured by the Federal government. Roger said he wishes that he could say that the government takeover of the U.S. Office was successful, but his conscience will not permit it! Harrell's greatest delight has been his entire family, including his parents, his wife, children, and their grandchildren. In addition to preaching and serving as an elder as portrayed on the next page, he was able to accumulate 1,500 hours of flying time, earning a commercial license and an instrument rating.

Bible Version Information: The Amplified Bible is used in practically every printed page, demanding scriptural authority. The KJV was used only on one or two pages--very little use! "Scripture taken from The Amplified Bible, Old Testament was copyrighted ©1965, 1987, by the Zondervan Corporation. The Amplified New Testament copyright ©1958, 1987, by the Lockman Foundation. Used by Permission."

Copyright © Edition 2020 *This is God's World: Listen As He Speaks To Us!* by Dr. Roger Harrell

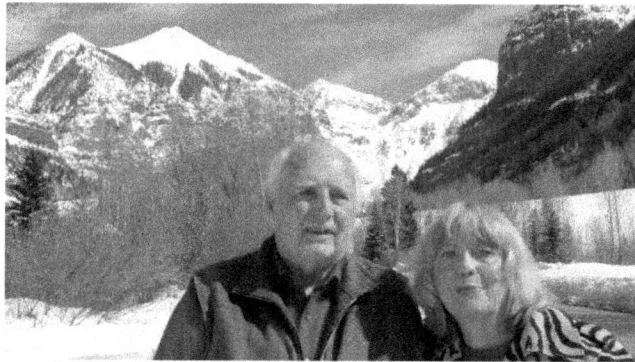

DR. ROGER L. HARRELL and DR. MARY ROSE HARRELL

ISBN 978057867990-7

All rights reserved solely by the Author. The author guarantees all content is original and does not infringe upon the legal rights of any person or work. No part of this book may be reproduced in any form without the permission of the author.

Unless otherwise indicated, Scripture quotations are taken from The Amplified Version Bible.

Professional Experiences And Intentions With The Book

This is a Biblical Adventure designed to assist the reader in the development of a Conceptual Framework for the Church, better yet, the Ekklesia that Jesus said He would build in Matthew 16:18, and continues to do so today. The Framework can then be used to assure anyone who may ask you to correctly address the message in the Introduction to 1st Peter. This message is one that all Christians should be able to provide to every person who may pose the question to him or her. The word Ekklesia may be a new one for your vocabulary! The word for Church in the Greek language, which Jesus would have spoken is ἐκκλησία, Greek alphabetization. From time to time we will use Ekklesia as it is in Greek. William Tyndale in A.D. 1526, prior to being strangled and burned at the stake in 1536, made this factual, as he translated the word Ekklesia, not to Church, rather in English, it translates to Congregation and/or Assembly, just as Jesus had wanted. It does make sense doesn't it?

Tyndale translated the Koine Greek to English. And this gave us one of our first such translations of the New Testament in English. We will leave no doubt about this factual matter. Beware of King James 1st, who changed the word Congregation to Church about 68 years following the printing of William Tyndale!

Author, Dr. Roger Harrell - Professional Experiences

Member, Board of Directors N.M.C.C.H.	Portales	NM	8 yrs.	Ret.
Assoc. Dean, Sch. of Educ. & Behav. Stu	Azusa	CA	4 yrs.	Ret.
Professor of Educational Admin. APU,	Azusa	CA	8 yrs.	Ret.
Superintendent of Schools	Monrovia	CA	6 yrs.	Ret.
Superintendent of Schools	Carlsbad	NM	12 yrs.	Ret.
U.S. Office of Education	Washington	DC	1 yr.	Ret.
U.S. Off. of Educ. Coord. of Title Programs	West Texas	TX	3 yrs.	Ret.
Texas A&M University-Assist Prof.	College Sta.	TX	3 yrs.	Ret.
Dir. Of Curric. And Instruc. Public Sch.	Santa Fe	NM	2 yrs.	Ret.
Public School Teaching, Bio., Chem., Physics	TX, CA, NM		14 yrs.	Ret.
Part-Time Minister; Seven years as an elder	TX & CA		10 yrs.	Ret.

Preface

Whether you are a college student, participate in a Bible Study or one that might not even have a relationship with God at this time, I think you will enjoy the excitement written into the pages of this book. For example, have you ever seen or discussed these words that are developed herein? It is in English, however, better described in Greek as Ekklesia (ἐκκλησία.), which translates into two words, Congregation and/or Assembly, not Church, as is currently done by several Bible Publishers, and I would guess about 95% of biblical study users. Hence, we have a huge readership of uneducated with regard to the Greek Language, using strictly English language. This would include: What did Jesus say He would build?

We look at issues of worship and ask the question, "How did so many folks escape, beginning in time (1) from right after New Testament Times, A.D. 1 forward, through the period of time that included A.D. 1525-26, wherein William Tyndale provided the New and Old Testaments, then (2) through the early and late colonial days, during the period of reformation and restoration, and to and through the times of what King James 1st and his Authorized Version--KJB, dated A.D. 1611 to (3) present times of Biblical Worship of God, and His Son Jesus Christ?" Fortunate were those who escaped the corruption that had broken out in the Big Churches (you can guess which ones) in a time that we will simply call Horrible. How did all of these men and women come up with so many ideas different from one another? Each church, of course, strongly shouts that this is the true word and pattern of worshiping God. And God, we pray that You will guide all of us to Truth! To try and answer this phenomenon in America, much less in the World, we will give due diligence to procedures used in worship services that will offer the readers a way of developing a conceptual framework of the church, better even yet, the congregation and/or assembly that Jesus said He would build and is still building. Did He really say, "I will build my church"? (Matt. 16:18) Let's think a while about that question! Times up! No! He did not say He would build His church per say, in English Language. Assuredly, however, He did say I will build my Congregation, or if the use of the word mandated it, one would be justified in saying I will build my Assembly. (Such as the Assembly in the Wilderness).

As long as it is present "I will build my ekklesia," and /or (ἐκκλησία), we will have a very good foundation. This word translates to Congregation and/or Assembly from ekklesia and/or ἐκκλησία from anyone. It takes fraud on man's watch to make it read as it could have been, once that it had been changed!

The understanding of how and what Jesus is now building will become the centerpiece for discussion as we study scripture throughout the book and truly give our lives to Christ as He would have us do. Yet, one will see an unfolding of words that may be used in our discussions that will relate to courteousness and respectfulness for another's point of view, while holding first to God's spoken words.

Special Thanks

To Dr. Steve Eckstein, Jr. and his wife Mildred. Dr. Eckstein was my professor of Bible at ENMU in Portales, New Mexico. Thank you, Dr. Eckstein for your thoughts and wishes on the book. I have taken a paragraph from one of your publications and used it in a special way to introduce the readers to the body of this subject matter. You are extremely knowledgeable in all matters of the ἐκκλησία of Christ and a world spokesman for God's Word. You have touched so many students! The touch of wisdom is a great gift from anyone, and it is no secret, what you and God have done! He has blessed you with clear thinking and great abilities in most every area of life. That blessing has been shared by so many people that we will have many things to discuss when we all get to Heaven! Thanks for all you have done.

To Mr. Dennis Moore, an elder of the Gateway Church of Christ in Ruidoso, New Mexico. Brother Moore, many people have received great information and encouragement from you, having been a former Minister of the ekklesia. I regard you as one of the top teachers of Biblical studies. Whether it is teaching or preaching, you are thorough, and inspire those sitting in class to partake in a feast of learning. You have offered me great guidance and encouragement with the book. Your wisdom is profound. Your concepts of Love and the whole duty of mankind are tremendous. You are truly a servant of His and will be rewarded as time continues. I appreciate the fact that you have a last chapter in my book. I know our readers will surely look forward to that time.

To Mr. John Duncan, Minister of the Gateway Church of Christ, you are a great preacher, and you have been of much assistance to me with thoughts about the King. This congregation of Christians is one that matches those of the busiest in God's work in any congregation that I have ever attended. You have made the book better with your relevant input and suggestions. The leadership you and the elders in your congregation provide will impact the membership for years to come. I believe that these men Love God, know His word very well, and will provide you with the type of ongoing Leadership that will assist you in the pulpit to be able to share with each non-Christian and Christians the complete account of the story of Hope that God left in His words of Wisdom, Direction and Correction.

Thanks to the members of the Eat and Talk Club, for your help in making this a better book. Hostess Mary Harrell and son John Harrell, Barney and Sonya Newton, Henry and Barbara Gossage, B.J. and Bob Wallace, James and Betty Withrow, Bonnie Chavez, Andy and Kitten Behrends, Les and Dolores Earwood, Lee Ann and Jerry Longbothom, and Joshua and Ashley Watkins. We pause to announce that one of our highly respected members passed away in February of 2016. She was Mrs. Kitten Behrends, wife of Mr. Andy Behrends. Kitten will be greatly missed by Andy and all of the members of this committee as it continues to meet occasionally for a discussion of materials and/or problems of the Body of Christ that may be encountered and/or addressed for considerations of solutions among the Body of Christ.

Foreword

You are about to engage in a Biblical experience that is designed for those who seek to serve Jesus Christ, our Redeemer and our Lord and Savior. The passage 1st Peter 3:15 serves as the main motivation in the development of this study!

This book will be informative to all and it is well suited for all religious groups, growing out of the early ἐκκλησία in N.T. times and the era when attempts were made to clear out the errors that had accumulated in what was called, the Catholic Church. This followed several centuries after Christ ascended to Heaven to be in His Kingdom at the Right Hand of God, His Father.

This happened as predicted in the Old Testament, Psalms 110. And the Apostle Peter around A.D. 63, said in 1st Peter 3:22, "[And He, Jesus] has now entered into Heaven and is at the right hand of God with [all] angels and authorities and powers made subservient to Him."

This is to be until such time that He would return for His Second Coming--the exact time, known Only by God--to take His faithful family of believers, those souls, who were once lost, including you and me! This includes transporting all of His obedient followers, to a better place, His Eternal Kingdom. (2nd Peter 1: 9-11) Please read this passage of scripture just mentioned. It is a Promise of protection to us for Eternal Life, providing we obey our Lord.

We will understand completely that the deal with sticks and stones was not **bold. Boldness is** rather Faith, Holiness, and God's Grand Love. But let's add to this God's grace, Mercy of Christ and His death upon the cross for our sins. This of course brought redemption and Eternal Life to all who sought after and claimed Jesus as their Savior in Obedience.

Dedication

This book is dedicated to my brilliant, beautiful, and loving wife, Dr. Mary Rose Harrell, our very amazing and gregarious stock trading son, John, who has helped Mary and I in our "getting older era." To our terrific, wise, and very smart and thoughtful daughter, Kelli, her gifted and caring husband Ben and their two very talented children, Oliver and Alexander, our grandchildren. To our other terrific, wise, and very smart and thoughtful daughter, Jill, her ambitious, patriotic, and loving husband Chris and their three smart and joyful children, Camille, Luke and Madeline, our grandchildren.

Mary joins me in saying, we have had the time of our lives raising three tremendous and loving children! It was fun and believe us, never a dull minute. Then there were the grandchildren. What another exciting time!

I want you to know that I have loved each one of you as much as any husband, father or grandfather possibly could.

I want each of you to have a fulfilling and happy Christian life! There will come a time when time no longer exists as we know it today. It will be a spectacular moment to be reunited with each of you again, as we will be with God, Christ, and the Holy Spirit for Eternity!

It's important to note that prior to my lifesaving surgery on April 22, 2020 in Mesa, AZ., I struggled with accelerating Vascular Dementia in writing this book. Due to greatly increased blood flow, the Dementia has now diminished significantly after a special procedure was performed by an amazing Cardiologist, Dr. Richard Heuser.

After my cardiologists in New Mexico told me there was nothing more they could do, my son John frantically searched the internet in hopes of finding someone that could provide a pathway through arteries whereby prior attempts at stenting were unsuccessful. God provided hope when John found a doctor who recently invented a device that stretches the arteries and allows them to be cleaned out. For that I am grateful. When the cardiologists were against trying this new procedure, my family doctor, Dr. Christopher Robinson, agreed with my son and said, "Go for it. What do you have to lose?" I am thankful for his push in helping me make a decision that ultimately saved my life.

John, thank you so much for your tenacity and desire to see my life extended. Thank you for four months of your time in editing and organizing my thoughts in preparation for the publication of this book.

Big Daddy Harrell
(September 2020)

Table of Contents

The Back and Front of this Book signify the beauty that God used in the Creation of the Earth and the Heavens. Photos were taken by Soul Hat (Mike Davis) and Mark Stambaugh Photography (Mark Stambaugh) in the mountains around Ruidoso, New Mexico.

Cover layout and design by GenevieveNicoleDesigns.com

Chapter One

Translation of Ekklesia by William Tyndale for Jesus Christ

I feel as though that we all are ready to be engaged in reading about William Tyndale in his battle with King James 1st, a battle that Tyndale never knew about, and one that most people in the world at the present time, have yet to hear about his huge problem! He, Tyndale, knew that he was asked to develop the first English Bible, from Greek text. It was called Koine Greek. The definition of Koine Greek may be quickly read on page (21) of this literature.

Tyndale was blessed by God and may well have been chosen by Him to help Jesus get started on the manuscript. This project was not necessarily an easy undertaking from start to go, never mind from start to completion. What we are attempting to show you at this point is that he understood Jesus. He loved Jesus. He helped those for whom he was writing. He was of the ordinary man and this did help as a man of God. After the capture of Tyndale and strangulation later by his captors, they set him on fire at the stake! What a pitiful way to dispose of his body at the stake. Tyndale was a great man who knew what it was to worship his Lord. May William Tyndale rest in peace in the hereafter!

Chapter and verse, Acts 17:24. It says, "God that made the worlde and all that are in it seynge that He is Lord of heven and erth he dwelleth not in temples made with honds." The reader has just witnessed a bit of the (original writing in Ole English) by William Tyndale, around A.D. 1525-26. This is some of Luke's writing, while in the presence of Paul. The following sections reveal 115 times that a word was meant to be **Congregacion** and/or **Assembly**, but we were now, 86 years later, from the date A.D. 1525-26. It meant **church.**

This word was **without doubt changed** from Tyndale's translation. Is this possible? Did not King James have the ability to know that Ole English was to the purposeful language of Christians in many areas at that time? The words were indeed **Congregacion** and/or **Assembly** and not the word **church.** King James spoiled it as Jesus had not wanted this to happen! The King knew better than to do what he did, but he had apparently no concern for what Jesus had indirectly assigned William Tyndale.

Furthermore, I am being a bit playful! This King James was a good student and he knew the root word **Kuriakon** was not the root word that Tyndale used to get the two words that would work very well to produce what Jesus had requested, that is,

Congregacion and/or **Assembly**, but not the word **church**!

This action taken by King James 1st, and some people in the right places and in the proper way in A.D. 1611 would produce for him a **church**. You will be introduced to some literature that will tend to curl your hair. This kind of behavior on the part of the King is known as Fraud in the books of many.

How Tyndale First Addressed Matt. 16:18 In His Translation

The following is the way Jesus, our Savior, wanted to announce what was to be written in **Matt. 16:18. "And I saye also vuto the yt thou arte Peter: and upon this rock I wyll byide my congregacion and/or assembly. And the gates of hell shall not prevayle ageynst it." Yes, William Tyndale wrote it correctly!**

Eighty-six years later, the words were actually changed when **Kuriakon** was used in order to get the word **church**, that King James 1st wanted. It is not valid unless a book writer and/or publisher want it to be that way? Yes, it is incorrect and thus wrong, but it needs to be shown to all of us who are ourselves Christians.

Matt 16:18 now looks like this. "And I say also unto thee, That thou art Peter and upon this rock I will build my church." It's Too Bad! King James 1st got what he wanted. What a difference a word makes! It has caused real troubles in the worship of Christ for many Christians! William Tyndale created a flawless **Congregacion** and/or **Assembly** from the God given word Ekklesia, as opposed to using the incorrect word, a derivative of Kuriakon for the word **church. [It doesn't fit the pattern.]** Does the word **Congregacion** and/or **Assembly** sound like a church building as we know churches throughout the world and particularly the beautiful structures as well as their possible locations?

Are we able to agree that a **Congregacion** (old spelling,) (new spelling-**Congregation**) and/or (**Assembly**) conveys to Christians, that which Christ said He was going to build? It is not the building that makes the difference, or is it? Isn't it a time to praise God and be with our brothers and sisters in Christ?

The Old English writings are sometimes very difficult to read. If you cannot read in spots in this chapter, go ahead, grab your Bible and you will be reading Old English in no time! Ninety-nine chances out of 100 you might be reading the word **church**. Why? King James the 1st was able to set it forth this way!

2

Overlook that and concentrate on re-living a life that had no big beautiful church; rather it had small buildings, wonderful men, women, boys and girls in attendance. You found yourself blessed and truly felt the brotherhood of people of God singing and making melody in their hearts, singing music and praising Jesus and God. You will also thank the Holy Spirit for assisting us in worshiping God and honoring Jesus our Savior!

How many times have you and I said on Sunday morning, "Hurry Up; It's time to go to **church**!" Isn't it really a time to praise God and give thanks to Him for His Son Jesus and the Holy Spirit?

Through the Scriptures in The Tyndale Bible: A.D. 1525-26

Matt. 16:18 And I say also unto the yt thou arte Peter: and upon this rocke I wyll byide my congregacion...

Acts 5:11 And great feare came on all the congregation and on as many as hearde it.

Acts 7:38 This is he that was in ye congregacion in the wyldernes with the Angell which spake to him in ye moute Syna and with oure fathers. This man receave the worde of lyfe to geve vnto.

Acts 8:1 And he kneled doune and cryed with a loude oynce: Lorde ay not this synne to their charge. And when he had thus spoken, he fell a slepe.

Saul had pleasure in his deeth. And at yt tyme there was a great persecucion against the congregacion which was at Jerusalem and they were all scattered abroade thorowout the regions of lury and Samaria except the Apostles.

Acts 8:3 But Saul made havocke of the congregacion entrynge into every housse and drew out bothe man and woman and thrust the into preson.

Acts 9:31 Then had ye congregacions rest thorowoute all lewry and galile and Samary and were edified and walked in the feare of the lorde and multiplied by the comforte of the holy gost.

Acts 11:22 Tydinges of these things came vnto ye eares of the congregacion which was in Ierusalem. And they sente for the Barnabas that he shuld go vnto Antioche.

Acts 11:26 And when he had founde him he brought him vnto Antioche. And it chaunsed yt a whole yere they had their conversation with the congregacion there and taught moche people: in so mouche that the disciples of Antioche were the fyrst that were called Christen.

Acts 12:1 In that tyme Herode the kynge stretched forth his handes to vexe certayne of the congregacion.

Acts 12:5 Then was Peter kepte preson. But prayer was made without ceasynge of the congregacion.

Acts 13:1 There were at Antioche in the congregacion certayne Prophetes and teachers: as Barnabas and Simon called Niger and Lucius of Cerene and Manahen Herode the Tetrarkes norsfellowe and Saul.

Acts 14:23 And when they had ordered them elders by eleccion in every congregacion after they had prayde and fasted they comended them to God on whom they believed.

Acts 14:27 When they were come and had gaddered the congregacion to gedder they rehearsed all that God had done by them and how he had opened the dore of faith vnto the getyls.

Acts 15:3-4 After they were brought on their waye by the congregacion they passed over Phenices and Samaria declarynge the conuersion of the getyls and they brought great ioye vuto all ye brethern. **v4** And when they were come to Ierusalem they were receaved of the congregacion and of the Apostles and elders. And they declared what Whinges Goddone by them.

Acts 15:22 Then pleased it the Apostles and elders wt the whole congregacion to sende chosyn men of their owne copany to Antioche with Paul and Barnabas. They sent Iudas called Barsabas and Silas which were chefe men amonge the brethre.

Acts 15:41 And he went thorowe all Cyria and Cilicia stablisshynge the congregacions.

Acts 16:5 And so were the congregacions stablisshed in the fayth and encreased in noumbre dayly.

4

Acts 18:22 and came vnto Cesarea: and ascended and saluted the congregacion and departed vnto Antioche.

Acts 19:32, 39, 41 Read verses **32** thru **38** for information that will add this set of scriptures and will provide background for **v39** and **v41**. You require anything further about this or other matters, it must be decided and cleared up in the regular **assembly**. (Yf ye goo about eny other thinge it may be determined in a lawful **assembly**.) **Verse 40** For we are in danger of being called to render an account and of being accused of rioting because of this commotion today, being no reason that we can offer to justify this disorder. **Verse 41** And when he had said these things, he dismissed the **assembly**.

The Greek Text is that of Stephens (1550), which has long been in common use, but as the edition of Elzevir (1624) is the one often called Received Text or Textus Receptus because of the words "Textum... ab omnibus receptum," we give the readings of the Elzevir edition in The Received Text. Again, this may be referred to as the Textus Receptus.

The preceding material will be useful to make acquaintance with it, allowing you to read some of the material that can be used as found in my material in this work, flowing from *The Interlinear Literal Translation of the Greek New Testament*, (Zondervan Publishing House, Grand Rapids, Michigan, 1966). Refer to page iii.

Returning to Tyndale's writing of scripture about A.D. 1525-26.

Acts 19:41 "And when He had said these things, he dismissed the assembly."

Just a few more words of elaboration! I assume you may be saying, Why? Simply said, it is because these verses do not really say anything that a civil, God Fearing person would honestly want to say! What was said or said about, came from another life of simplicity! A choice that so far, most people have found a really easy thing to do. What is it? It's like drinking one's self to oblivion before the effect of the substance is even really known. It leaks into one's activities that sort of get out of control and the Devil becomes in full control as you are more out of control. The substance is **alcoholic**, but most people from age 5 or 6 should begin to quickly understand why they never want to really get mixed into this substance, which leads to unbelievable activities and hurtful days. Please please Watch, Guide and Protect your children.

Acts 20:17 Wherefore from Myleton he sent to Ephesus and called the elders of the congregation.

Acts 20:28 Take head therefore vnto youre selves and to the flocke whereof the holy goost hath made youer ears to rule the congregacion of God whic he hath purchas.

Rom. 16:1 I commede vnto Phebe oure sister (which is a deaconess of the congregacion (of the Christians at her house) of Chenchrea)

Rom. 16:4 which have for my lyfe layde their awne neckes. Vnto which not I only geve thankes but also the congregacion of the getyls.

Rom. 16:16 Salute one another with an holy kysse. The congregacion of Christ salute you.

Rom. 16:23 Gaiu myne host ean the hoste of all the congregacions saluteth you. Erastus the chamberlayne of ye cite saluteth you. And Quartus a Brother.

1 Cor. 1:2 Vnto the congregacion of God which is at Corinthum. To them that are sanctified in Christ Iesus by calling with all that call on the name of oure Lord Iesus Christ in every place both of theirs and of ours.

1 Cor. 4:17 For this cause have I sent vnto you Timotheus which is my deare sonne and faithful in the Lorde which shall put you in remembrauce of my wayes which I have in Christ eve as I teache everwhere in all congregacions.

1 Cor. 6:4 If ye have judgementes of worldely matters take them which are despised in ye congregacion and make them judges.

1 Cor. 7:17 the Lorde...called every person...so orden I in all congregacions.

1 Cor. 10:32 Se that ye geve occasion of evell nether to ye Iewes nor yet to ye congregacion of God.

1 Cor. 11:16 If there be eny man amonge you yt lusteth to stryve let him knowe that we have no souche custome nether the congregacions of God.

1 Cor. 11:18 Fyrst of all when ye come togedder in the congregacion I heare that ther is dissencion amonge you: and I partly believe it.

1 Cor. 11:22 Or els despyse ye the congregacion of God and shame them that have not? What shall I saye vnto you? shall I prayse you: In this prayse I you not.

1 Cor. 12:28 And God hath also ordeyned in the congregacion fyrst the Apostles secodarely prophets thyrdly teachers then the that do miracles: after that the gyftes of healing helpers governers diversite of tonges.

1 Cor. 14:4-5 He that speaketh with tonges proffiteth him silfe he that prophesyeth edifieth the congregacion. **v5** I wolde that ye spake with tonges: but rather that ye prophesied. For greater is he that prophisieth then he yt speaketh with tonges except he expounde it also that the congrgacion maye have edifyinge.

1 Cor. 14:12 Eve so ye (for as moche as ye covet spreteuall giftes) seke that ye maybe have plentye vnto ye edifyinge of the congregacion.

1 Cor. 14:19 Yet had I lever inye congregacion to speake five wordes with my mynde to ye informacion of other rather then ten thousande wordes wt the tonge.

1 Cor. 14:23 Yf therefore when all the congregacion is come to gedder and all speake with tonges ther come in they yt are vnlearned or they which believe not will they not saye that ye are out of youre wittes?

1 Cor. 14:28 But yf ther be no interpreter let him kepe silence in the congregation and let him speake to himselfe and to God.

1 Cor. 14: 33-35 (v33) For God is not causer of stryfe: but of peace as he is in all other congregacions of the saynctes **(v34)** Let your wyves kepe silence in the congregacions. For it is not permitted vnto them to speake: but let them vnder obedience as sayth the lawe. **(v35)** If they will learne enythinge let the axe their husbandes at home. For it is a shame for wemen to speake in the congregacion.

1 Cor. 15:9 For I am the lest of all the Apostles which am not worthy to be called an Apostle because I persecuted the congregacion of God.

1 Cor. 16:1 Of the gadderynge for the saynctes as I have ordeyned in the congregacions of Galacia even so do ye.

1 Cor. 16:19 The congregacions of Asia salute you. Aquila and Priscilla salute you mouch in the Lorde and so doeth the congregacion that is in their housse.

1 Cor. 1:1 Paul an Apostle of Iesus Christ by the will of God and brother Timotheus. Vnto the congregacion of God which is at Corinthu with all the saynctes which are in all Achaia.

2 Cor. 8:1 I do you to wit brethren of the grace of God which is geven in the congregacions Macedonia.

2 Cor. 8: 18-19 We haue sent with him that brother whose laude is in the gospel thorow out all the congregacions: **v19** and not so only but is also chosen of the congregacion to be felowe with vs in oure iorney concerninge this benevolence that is ministred by vs vnto the prayse of ye lorde and to stere vp youre prompt mynde.

2 Cor. 8:23-24 hath caused me this to do: partly for Titus sake which is my felowe and helper as cocernynge you partly because of other which are oure Brethren and the messengers of the congregacions and ye glory of Christ. **v24** Wherfore shewe vnto them the proffe of youre love and of the rioysynge that we have of you that ye congregacions maye se it.

2 Cor. 11:8 I robbed other congregacions and toke wages of the to do you service with all.

2 Cor. 11:28 And beside the thynges which outwardly happe vnto me I am cobred dayly and do care for all congregacions.

2 Cor. 12:13 For what is it wherin ye were inferiors vnto other congregacions except it be ther that I was not greveous vnto you. Forgive me this wronge done vnto you.

Gal. 1:2 and all the brethren which ar with me. Vnto the congregacions Galacia.

Gal. 1:13 For ye have hearde of my conversacion in tyme past in the Iewes ways how that beyond measure I persecuted the congregacion of God and spoyled it.

Gal. 1:22 and was vnknowen as touchinge my person vnto ye congregacion of Iewrye which were in Christ.

Eph. 1:22 and hath all thynges vnder his fete and hath made him aboue all thynges ye heed of ye congregacion.

Eph. 3:10 to the intent that now vnto the rulars and powers in heven might be knowe by the congregacion ye many flode wisdome of God.

Eph. 3:21 be prayse in the congregacion by Iesus Christ thorow out all generacious from tyme Amen.

Eph. 5:23-25 For the husbande is the wyves heed even as Christ is the heed of the congregacion and the same is the saveoure of [is] Body,

v24 Therefore as the congregacion is in subieccion to Christ lykwyse let the wyves be in subieccion to their husbandes in all thing **v25** Husbandes love youre wyves even as Christ loved the congregacion and gave him silfe for her.

Eph. 5:27 to make it vnto him selfe a glorious congregacion with oute spot or, wrynckle or eny soche thinge: but that it shuld be holy and without blame.

Eph. 5:29 For no ma ever yet hated his awne fless he: but norisshe and cherissdeth it even as the lorde doth the congregacion.

Eph. 5:32 This is a great secrete but I speake bitwene Christ and the congregacion.

Phil. 3:6 and as concernynge fervetnes I perseuted the congregacion and as touchynge the rightewesnes which is in the lawe I was vnrebukable.

Phil. 4:15 Ye Philippos know that in the begynnynge of the gospel when I departed from Macedonia no congregacion bare parte with me as concernynge gevynge and receavynge but ye only.

Col. 1:18 And he is the heed of the body that is to wit of the congregacion: he is the begynnynge and fyrst begotten of the deed that in all thynges he might have the preeminence.

Col. 1:24 Now ioye in my soferinges which I suffre for you and fulfill that which is behynde of the passions of Christ in my flesshe for his bodies sake which is the congregacion.

Col. 4:15-16 Salute the brethren which are of Laodicia and salute Nymphas and the congregacion which is in his house **v16** And whe the pistle is reed of you make that it be reed in the congregacion of the Laodicians also: and that ye lyke wyse reed ye epistle of Laodicia.

1 Thes. 1:1 Paul Syluanus and Timotheus. Vnto the congregacion of the Tessalonyans in God the father and ye Lorde Iesus Christ. Grace be with you and peace from God oure father and the Lorde Iesus Christ.

1 Thes. 2:14 For ye brethren became followers of the congregacion of God which in Iewry are in Christ Iesus: for ye have suffered lyke thynges of youre kynsmen as we oure selves have of the Iews.

1 Thes. 1:1 Paul Syluanus and Timotheus. Vnto the congregacion of the Tessalonyans which are in God oure father and in the Lorde Iesus Christ.

2 Thes. 1:4 so yt we oureselves reioyce of you in the congregacions of God over youre pacience and fayth in all youre persecucions and tribulacios that ye suffer.

1 Tim. 3:5 For if a man cannot rule his owne housse how shall he care for the congregacion of God?

1 Tim. 3:15 but and yf I tarie longe yt then thou mayst yet have knowledge how thou oughtest to behave thy silfe in the housse of God which is the congregacion of the living God the pillar and grounde of trueth.

1 Tim. 5:16 And yf eny man or woman that beleveth have widdows let the minister vnto them and let not the congregacion be charged: that yt maye have sufficient for them that are widdowesd in dede.

Philem. 1:2 and to the beloved Appia and to Archippus oure felowe soudier and to the congregacion of [that meets in] your house.

Heb. 2:12 ayinge: I will declare thy name vnto my brethren and in me myddes of the congregacion will I prayse the.

Heb. 12:23 and vnto the congregacion of ye fyrst borne sonnes which are writte in heven and to God the iudge of all and to the spretes of iust and parfecte men.

James 5:14 Yf eny be defeated amonge you let him call for the elders of the congregacion and let the praye over him and anoynte him with oyle in the name of the lorde:

3 John 1:6 which bare witness of thy love before all the congregacion. Which brethren whe thou bryngest forwardes on their iorney (as it besemeth God) thou shalt do well.

3 John 1:9-10 I wrote vnto the congregacion: but Diotrephes which loveth to have the preeminence amoge them receaveth vs not. **v10** Wherfore yf I come I will declare his dedes which he doeth iestinge on vs with malicious wordes nether is therewith content. Not only he him silfe receaveth not the brethre: but also he forbiddeth them that wolde and thrusteth out of the congregacion.

Rev. 1:4 Ihon to the vii congregacions in Asia. Grace be with you and peace from him which is and which was and which is to come and from the seven spretes .vii.

Rev. 1:11 Ihon to the vii congregacions in Asia. Grace be with you and peace from him which is and which is was and which is to come and from the, vii. spretes which are present before his trone spretes which are present before his trone.

Rev. 1:20 and ye mystery of the vii Stares which thou sawest in my ryght honde and the vii golden candlestyckes. The vii stares are the messengers of the vii congregacions: And the vii candlestyckes which thou sawest are the vii congregacions.

Rev. 2:1 Unto the messenger of the congregacion of Ephesus wryte: these thynges sayth he that holdeth the vii. Stares in his right honde and walketh in the myddes of the vii golden candlestyckes.

Rev. 2:7-8 Let him yt hath eares heare what ye sprete sayth vnto the congregacions. To him that overcometh will I geve to eate of the tree of lyfe which is in the myddes of ye paradice of God **v8** And vnto the angell of the congregacion of Smyrna wryte: These thynges sayth he that is fyrst and the laste which was deed and is alive.

Rev. 2:11-12 Let him that hath eares heare what the sprete sayth to the congregacions: he that overcometh shall not be hurte of the seconde deeth. **v12** And to the messenger of the congregacion in Pergamos wryte: This sayth he which hath ye sharpe swearde with two edges.

Rev. 2:17-18 Lett him that hath ears heare what the sprete sayth vnto the congregacions: To him that over commeth will I give to eate manna that if hydn will geve him a whyte stone and in the stone a newe name written which no man knoweth saving ehe that receave thit. **(v18)** And vn to the messenger of the congregacion of Theatir write: This sayth the sonne ofGod which hath his eyes lyke vnto a flame offyre whose fete are like brasse.

Rev. 2:23 And I will Kyll her children with deeth. And all the congregacions shall knowe that I am he which searcheth ye reynes and hertes. And I will geve vnto evere one of you accordynge vnto youre workes.

Rev. 2:29 Let him yt hath eares heare what the sprete sayth to the congregacions.

Rev. 3:1 And wryte vnto the messenger of the congregacion of Sardis: this sayth he that hath the sprete of God and the vii. starres. I knowe thy workes thou haste a name that thou lvyest and thou art deed.

Rev. 3:6-7 Let him that hath eares heare what the sprete sayth vnto the congregacions. **v7** And wryte vnto ye tydinges bringer of ye congregacion of Philadelphia: this sayth he yt is holy and true which hath ye keye of Dauid: which openyth and no ma shutteth and no ma openeth.

Rev. 3:13-14 Let him that hath eares heare what the sprete sayth vnto the congregacions. **v14** (And) vnto the messenger of ye congregacion which is in Laodicia wryte: This sayth (ame) the faythfull and true witness ye begynninge of the creatures of God.

Rev. 3:22 Let him yt hath eares heare what the sprete sayth vnto the congregacions.

Rev. 22:16 I Iesus sent myne angell to testyfye vnto you these thynge in the congregacions. I am the rote and the generacion of David and the bright mornynge starre.

Thus, the end of some of the first mentioned words of Jesus Christ for communications to the world using the best of teachers and the translator, William Tyndale. After reading this material have you said to yourself, "These are truly the words from the Son of God?"

More About Early Writings With Relevancy To Christ

Examples of the Greek Text that was Stephens (1550) have long been in common use, but the edition of Elzevir (1624) is the one often called Received text or Textus Receptus because of the words "Textum....Ab omnibus receptum." It is the text commonly reprinted on the Continent. In the main they are one and the same, and either of them may be referred to as the Textus Receptus.

Samples follow of the Interlinear Literal Translation of the Greek New Testament with the King James Authorized Version. Following Stephens and/or Elzevir, authors of Textus Receptus writings will provide you a feeling for how the language changed in times from that of William Tyndale (Author of the first Greek published scriptures) as shown on the opening page of this paper, called William Tyndale Writes (A.D. 1525-26).

From The Textus Receptus

Acts 17:24 The God who made the world and all things that [are] in it, He of heaven and earth Lord being, not in hand-made temples dwells,

Matt. 16:18 And I also to thee say, That thou art Peter, and on this rock I will build my **Assembly**, and gates of hades shall not prevail against it.

Gal.1:22 And all the Brethren which are with me unto the **assemblies of...**

Eph. 5:27 That he might present it to himself a glorious **assembly**, not having spot or wrinkle, or any such thing; but that it should be holy.

Rev. 22:16 Jesus have sent mine angel to testify unto you these things in the **assemblies.** I am the root and the Offspring of David and the bright and Morning Star.

It takes only a quick glance to recognize that the word church was never mentioned above, even though the writing by William Tyndale was a distant number of years from his first writing as per request by Jesus our Lord.

Finally, we finish a brief description of words that the speakers used containing the word **Church**. When you see this word **Church**, please understand that this is not what Jesus or whoever was speaking with authority from Jesus and or God, requested! After seeing the word **Church** in this ill written version of the King James, real input, let me know of your feeling about what the King really did.

From The King James Bible-Authorized Version

Acts 17:24 God that made the World and all things therein, seeing that He is Lord of Heaven and earth, dwelleth not in temples made with hands.

Matt. 16:18 And I say unto thee That though art Peter and upon this rock I will build my **church**, and the gates of hell shall not prevail against it.

1 Cor. 7:17 But as God has distributed to every man as the Lord hath called everyone, so let him walk, and so ordain I in all **churches**.

Gal. 1:22 And was unknown by face unto the **churches** of Judea which were in Christ.

Eph. 5:2 that he might present it to himself a glorious **church**, not having spot or wrinkle or any such thing; but that it should be Holy without blemish.

Rev. 22:16 I Jesus have sent my messenger (angel) to testify unto you these things in the churches (assemblies). I am the root and the offspring of David, and the bright and morning star.

The Purpose of the first 16 pages in this chapter was to assist the readers in trying to show that King James 1st and his followers did a very foolish thing by rejecting what was inserted by Tyndale in translating the New Testament as Jesus' spokesperson had translated it, as had been requested.

That is, leave Ekklesia alone so that the manuscript when Congregation and/or Assembly words were needed, Ekklesia would correctly address what Jesus had said. William Tyndale had written in A.D. 1525-26 what Jesus and His Father wanted. His original charge for English speakers was to develop a phrase of mighty words or sayings in a modified Koine Greek form, "I will build my ekklesia." Let's do a quick review.

Tyndale was successful. Thanks be to God! The word Ekklesia would only translate to one of two words, **Assembly** and/or **Congregacion**. The word that was changed by King James' translators was the word Kuriakon, used 1500 to 2500 years before Christ was born in the Jerusalem area. There was cheating to do it this way for the following reason. Ekklesia (ἐκκλησία)) was not compatible with Kuriakon. The translators for King James would have understood, "not to use that which had changed from language to language." This would be much like a runner on third base trying to score on a sacrifice fly. He can't leave the base until the ball is caught, yet he did. What did the umpire say? You're out!

Chapter Two

Our Times: Strengths Or Weaknesses?

How can we get the thoughts of readers and listeners of what has really been bothering them? We Pondered, We shouted, We Answered them! Let's hear what they have to say. We asked them, and here is what they said! It was something that I had given thought, but not nearly enough. This just may be the problem of our times, and we have just not realized it! Why? It involves eternity, or at least it could in a big way. God told us to watch and beware, but apparently we failed as civilized and uncivilized communities. To paraphrase, Jesus may have said, Be aware of those who would dare to stoop so low as to change the Gospel of Christ. Their awareness was not close to being sufficient and I can hear my Lord saying, "Oh foolish ones. Why?" Jesus may have thought, Why did you want to change the Gospel? Was your news better than the pattern of news that I left with you? I refer again to **Matt. 16:18**. It is a passage of scripture that almost all of us have known, believed and practiced. We have believed that Jesus said, "...I will build my **church**..." Upon further study, I am 100% sure that He did not say this! Here is what He did say in Greek about the **(ekklesia) (ἐκκλησία)** in English! When this word, Ekklesia, was in a language, Koine Greek to be sure, Jesus was familiar with it and knew that it is pronounced as ekklesia, **(ἐκκλησία).** It appears as the word that you see. This Greek word, as you well know, was translated into English by William Tyndale in A.D. 1525-26. This Greek word, **(ἐκκλησία)** translates directly to two English words, **Assembly** and/or **Congregacion**, and believe it or not, NOT to the word **church**. Christ wrote, or had it written exactly as He and His Father wanted it! Who would thwart it? The mystery, although it has taken many many years, has been solved! Or, has it? Very few out of billions of people have ever heard of this story. Is it being deliberately silenced? Do too many have too much to expose? In most of the English Bibles of today, the Greek word "**ekklesia**" is translated in most places as the word, "**church**." According to Jesus, it should not be translated to anything except "**ἐκκλησία.**" The English word "ekklesia" is found in 115 places in the New Testament. We witnessed this in Chapter One and we failed to see any word in the Bibles reviewed that had been translated from Greek to English as the word "**church**" in the New Testament. Isn't this proof enough? King James 1st said do it and it was done! What a shame! The roles are played in rulership capacities. Something went astray and most people know it, yet will not admit it.

The following material, pg. 30-31 is presented by: Cooper P. Abrams III. Mr. Abrams is currently Pastor of Calvary Baptist Church, Tremonton, Utah. (All End

Note numbers refer to the End Notes in Abrams' original text.) Christians must respond. [http://Calvary Baptist church.org]

In about 1000 B.C. and in Greek, the word "ekklesia" in this period of time meant, "a called out assembly of citizens summoned by the crier in a legislative assembly." (End Note 1) [See the Bibliography with End Notes 1 and 6] Ekklesia (ἐκκλησία) as used in the New Testament is taken from the root of this word which simply means to "call out."

The English dictionary reveals that the "English word "church," which is used incorrectly in our English Bible is taken from the late Greek word kyriakon, not ekklesia." (2) Ibid. [See End Note 2] The Greek word kyriakon is not found in the New Testament, "however in the New Testament the word used for a called-out assembly is the word ekklesia." The word Kuriakos is a noun and is used twice and found and in 1 Cor. 11:20 "the Lord's (kuriakos) supper (deipnon)." Revelation 1:10 reads, "the Lord's (Kuriakos) day (hemera.") The word "kuriakos" comes from the word "ku-ri-os," which means "Lord." The word kuriakos (i.e. church) means "pertaining to the Lord." Then this points to something that pertains to or belongs to a Lord. The Greek kuriakon eventually came to be used in Old English form as "cirice" (Kee-ree-ke), then "churche" (kerke), and eventually to mean "church" as a building. The Pocket Oxford English Dictionary provides us with the modern definition of church. 1. a building used for public worship. 2. a particular Christian organization. 3. The Christian religion as an institution with political or social influence. Origen from the Greek- Kuriakon doma 'Lord's house' (7) Ibid. [See End Note 7.] The word kuriakon (i.e. church) then, is correctly referred to as the "house of the Lord," meaning the building. This is a different meaning than the word ekklesia, which means a called-out assembly and/or congregation. As stated earlier the word "ekklesia" in itself does not explain who is meeting, but only as a group, it is to assemble. The context of the passage tells who is meeting. For example, the word ekklesia, is used in Acts 19:32, 39, 41 and demonstrates this word was used to refer to a civil assembly of local towns people of Ephesus which included idol makers.

Acts 19:24-25 records that a man named Demetrius called all workman of like occupations together for a meeting to discuss the problem. v39 indicates "the assembly was confused." The word assembly is from the Greek word ἐκκλησία from Koine Greek, into English as ekklesia and may be properly translated to **Assembly** and/or **Congregacion**.

Another example found in Acts 7:38 refers to the nation of Israel that was congregated at Mt. Sinai as the "church in the wilderness." The word translated as Church is the Greek word ekklesia. It is incorrect to refer to Israel as a Church and the word should be properly translated Assembly and or Congregacion.

In most places in the New Testament the word ekklesia refers to a local assembly of believers in Jesus Christ and should be accurately translated **Assembly or Congregacion.** Brown states that the word is limited in use to a particular geographical location: (3) Ibid. [See End Note 3.]

Selected Bibliography With End Notes

Collected by Cooper P Abrams III. For his computerized paper, The Translations of the Greek Word, "Ekklesia," as "church" in the English Bible and its Ramifications. All Rights Reserved. Pastor of Calvary Baptist Church-

Tremonton, Utah (Calvarybaptistchurch.org)

End Note 1. Webster's Universal College (New York: Gramercy, 1997), p.143.
End Note 2. R. Scott, and H. G. Liddell, A Greek-English Lexicon (Grand Rapids: Baker), p. 206
End Note 3. Brown, Colin. The New International Dictionary of New Testament Theology 3 vols. (Grand Rapids:1979), p. 291
End Note 6. Webster's Universal College (New York: Gramercy, 1997), p.143
End Note 7. Catherine Soanes, with Sara Hawker and Julia Elliott, Pocket Oxford Dictionary, Tenth Edition, (Oxford: Oxford University Press), 2005 p. 153

Faith-Holiness-Love

Love is all about God, Christ, The Holy Spirit, Christians and whether or not we follow someone else's directions or those from our Lord and Savior, Jesus Christ. This happens to be you, me, and all who exhibit their obedience to God by understanding the significance of Christ's teachings. Upon gaining his understanding, which is the essence of God's message to all mankind, Faith, Holiness, and Love, we become the mature goal, set forth by God and His Son, Jesus Christ! And having been redeemed, through obedience to His word, and through water immersion we look forward to spending eternity with our brothers and sisters in Christ.

By patiently awaiting for others to find their way to the invention of the printing press in the mid 1400's and forward and the additional explosive add-ons to the presses around the world, we have been enabled to read what the Lord Himself penned for us and to understand its ramifications in full!

You must know for certain that Jesus said what He had intended to say, exactly as He wanted it. Tyndale translated it correctly according to what Jesus had said! In short, He said, "I will build my ἐκκλησία," that is to say, I will build my **Congregacion** and/or **Assembly**. There is no doubt at all! It was King James 1st who so rudely ALTERED that which our Lord had caused to be written! Shortly before 1611, King James authorized himself to secure his wishes rather than leave standing what Jesus had already done in full measure, exactly as He had wanted it. The King ordered his translators of the new King James Bible (Authorized Version) to change the words such as in Article 3 in his list of 15 rules that translators were to follow, as they executed what King James wanted, namely, that he did not want any more language in the KJB(AV) that would be in conflict with his own personal thinking, declaring, **"the word church should not be associated with the Koine Greek word, Ekklesia, English pronunciation, in Greek as ἐκκλησία. Here are the direct words from the King's mouth. "The old Ecclesiastical words to be kept, viz. the word Church not to be translated as the ἐκκλησία."** In short, that is the story line. Amplification is to say, King James undoubtedly knew of the Ecclesiastical word kuriakon, the word for church, to show that he had knowledge of same. Recall that on page 39 in my first book, I called attention to work done by a brother in Christ, Dr. Stanley Morris, an expert by training in the languages of Hebrew and Greek, including Koine Greek, and quote Dr. Morrison this page and the next as having said, "Therefore the word church, though familiar, is not an accurate translation." These remarks came from the Christian Chronicle dated February 25, 2015.

Do you believe with all your heart and soul that King James 1st asked the translators of his KJB (Authorized Version) to follow his commands and respond to his instructions as he had directed in Article 3 in his list of 15 rules as valid fulfillment to his request? If you say Yes, I believe that you are right. If you say no, I believe you are wrong. If you said no at this point, you may never agree with what I and thousands of others truly believe. Yet, if you have not studied the issue, nor will you ever study the issue, you will continue to say, the word **church**. It is that simple! You will not find a legitimate word in Greek in the Bible, which you and I use every day, that permits us to legitimately say that Christ has built His **church. He did not want a church. He wanted a Congregation and/or Assembly, one that would agree with the structure and energy of the word ἐκκλησία.**

The question really becomes, will you and I and others have the strength and/or the ability to search the literature? I sense that you are going to ask a Question! Please! Be my guest. And you ask me! "Are you really saying that if I don't buy a Bible that truly has the words that Jesus wanted in that Bible, namely **Congregacion** and **Assembly** that I am going to Hell?" No, I did not say this, nor did it even cross my mind! If you are a Christian now, why would you be concerned that knowing, suddenly changes this? All that I can legitimately say is what I have said. Jesus did not say, nor did He want to say, "I will build my **church**." He did not use the wrong words that brought this about. He used the words at His command and said what He wanted to say. Have you ever wondered why Jesus, The Master Teacher and our Savior, from God's Book of Life, kept advising us, those of yesteryear and those of coming years, to be alert, to watch and make sure that no one brings about changes by not obeying the words used to prevent just this sort of thing? I must confess that I never really gave enough thought to this very question that I just asked you as I was growing into manhood! Praise God, I finally have!

Reactions: No! The word church as the world uses it today should not be in the bible! Now you know why I had a bit of room to become somewhat upset! But I take full responsibility. It struck me that nothing I said made much difference to the members, including ministers and elders from the congregations where I attended. I kept hearing the words, "Good Morning **church**," as if this was more for my ears than the ones speaking, or for the congregation. Then I thought how very silly I am to think just as they. For when I first learned of all of this, I could not believe it! As soon as I came to my senses, I realized that the Christian feels a necessity to be on guard at this very moment. It makes Christians feel that they must be on guard for Jesus. It was to help in this unending brawl with anyone who speaks about my Lord. Had He wanted to use the word **church**, He would have used the Greek derivation Kyriakos, a Greek Word for Lord, Kyrios implying Power!

Politics! Yes! But the fact is that the word **church** does not legitimately appear in the New Testament. This is an old ecclesiastical strain of Greek in use, prior to the birth of our Savior on earth. Jesus could have used it if that is what He and God had wanted to do. Factually, Jesus did not choose **church** as a name. If so, I cannot trace it down!

The following materials are referred to as being part of A or B below. Each will be followed by correct example:

A. Matt. 16:18 Jesus said, "...I will build my ἐκκλησία..." which directly translates in English, only to Congregacion and/or Assembly, "and the gates of Hell shall not prevail against it."

B. Matt. 16:18 Jesus said, "...I will build my 'church' And the gates of Hell shall not prevail against it..." Remember, the Greek word in your Bible is ekklesia and it translates directly, only to **Congregacion** and/or **Assembly**. It in no way could have correctly been translated into 'church' (Except with some manipulations ordered by King James 1st). It hurts me so much to say this!

A) Acts 7:38 Your Bible is ekklesia and it translates to **Assembly** and/or **Congregacion**, nothing else. "This is He who in the Assembly in the Wilderness (desert) was the go-between for the Angel..." It does not translate directly to the **church**!

B) Acts 7:38 "...This is He who was in the 'church' in the wilderness with the angel who spake with him." Remember, the Greek word in your Bible is ekklesia, and it translates directly to **Assembly** and/or **Congregacion**, not **church**.

If we proceed through the whole Bible where the word **church** appears as above for 115 times, the only thing that could or would be different would be the amount of paper that would be consumed in repeating the above for 115 times. I believe that we as a Body of Christ have the problem before us with meaningful questions to be thrown at us. We have problems aching to be resolved; however, we don't really know which one deserves to be resolved first do we, or do we? Why not nominate the item that we include that we believe needs to be resolved first?

Think for a moment of William Tyndale's part, and other early writers in the translations of "I will build my ἐκκλησία..." The evidence is such that little or no more research will have to occur to say without reservation our Savior has in mind a different message than now occurs.

Fraudulent and unwise statements were made or caused to be made at the request of King James to the translators he hired and used in denying the use of language that Jesus chose and had used in Matt.16:18. Jesus was honestly satisfied with the initial translation by William Tyndale, in which He said, "I will build My ἐκκλησία..." (translated to read as **My Congregacion and/or Assembly**).

One possibility is to study and resolve that most New Testaments in the USA are incorrectly translated in at least 115 places dealing with the word, "ἐκκλησία," and deliberately decide that we do or do not first need to establish the truth in our hearts as Jesus has shown, regarding the meaning of the ekklesia (in English from Koine Greek.)

Another possibility might be to discuss the merits of starting a movement of truth to provide friends and a multitude of many others, information to show that Jesus Christ, our

Savior, was correct when He used, in translating part of Matt. 16:18, the words that said, "I will build My ἐκκλησία," this word then translating to either, **Congregacion** and/or **Assembly**.

Someone might ask, what do ministers and/or elders in congregacions of today say when you try to get them to use the correct words in English, especially not **Church**, rather **Congregacion** or **Assembly**? That word pretty much is the all-time favorite. First of all, 99% of our fellow Christians, including the leadership element will have never known or heard of this, so they will not recognize that it is incorrect to use the word **church** in the Bible! Why? It messes with the word of God, and importantly the word for **church** is not in the Bible, per se. However, did He not warn us with scripture while He was here on earth? Heaven as He knows it will be? Yes, He warned us in scripture not to let anyone upset His wishes and try to follow a new path toward Heaven by changing the words that He left us as guides to follow!

These correct words are: English Translation--Ekklesia, translated as ἐκκλησία, from Koine Greek, a noun referred to as the Koine, an amalgam of Greek dialects, chiefly Attic and Ionic, that replaced the Classical Greek dialects in the Hellenistic period and flourished under the Roman Empire. (Taken from the Webster's Encyclopedic An Abridged Dictionary of the English Language, page 793.)

Honestly, most of the members will say **church** more loudly than usual after someone exposes them to this! Many are afraid of it! Another reality is, I believe, most of them do not really believe that all of this is really beginning to happen. They are convinced that "this too shall pass!"

What do I now say when asked to pray to our God in or out of my local congregacion? I never use any word that resembles **church** in English, other than ἐκκλησία, translating of course to **Congregation** or **Assembly**. The word ἐκκλησία is absent in almost all Bibles that are placed in or under the seats for the convenience of our visitors! In the United States of America, I could not begin to estimate how many Bibles there are in existence, which do not have what Jesus wanted, that is "word use" that compels attention to **Congregacion** and/or **Assembly**!

They wanted the precious words of so many new converts to the Lord. They wanted to hear the words **Congregacion** and/or **Assembly**. William Tyndale had written them in A.D. 1525-26, just as Jesus had requested. The rest is known! Jesus had written in His Koine Greek what He wanted to say to Billions of people with ready hearts and open eyes.

This undertaking was very successfully completed and survived, waiting of course, on the printing press (late 1400's to 1500's till now.)

Please keep in mind: This book was created just for you and me, and every person who wishes is invited to ascertain what we, individually must do to get the full benefit from Jesus who requested that it be written as it was before it was changed by King James 1st. You will begin to silently say Thank you, Jesus! Thank you! You will recall that Jesus really used the word, ἐκκλησία, ekklesia that may only be translated correctly into English from Koine Greek, into one of two words, when He said "...I will build My Congregacion and/or My Assembly." It also has a look of hypocrisy! Why? Hold your breath. If we do what Jesus directed in the name of the Kingdom of Christ, and/or Body of Christ, we would have to say that all members of the current Churches of Christ are really members of the Body of Christ. Now, we could say **Congregacions** of Christ and/or the **Assemblies** of Christ. Why? Because Jesus apparently wanted what He said, that being a **Congregacion** or **Assembly** of Christians. Don't forget! Had not King James 1st changed the word **Congregacion** and/or **Assembly** to **church**, and He did, don't ever say that our words as humans override the words and direction of our Lord and Savior, Jesus Christ, our Messiah. **Do We Stand Up For Jesus--Do We Sit Down--Or Both?** Perhaps we can stand and do the work that we Believe that Jesus would have us to do. And when we become tired, we can sit down and rest and refresh our lives with thoughts that lead to our eternity. This completion of **Two Items** 1.) Stand and work for Jesus, or 2). Rest and contemplate our thoughts that lead to eternity …. makes me believe that God will lead us to **Heavenly** places that are currently being built for **both you** and **me** and all who obey, and who may attempt to secure the **Biblical Knowledge** that we have been given and continue to learn ALL the truth! This truth can be gained from **God**, **Christ Jesus** and the **Holy Spirit!** I keep reading and hearing some of the following statements that give me great pleasure and hope. I adore the Lord Jesus as My Savior. It is a sign to me, and I believe to every human inhabitant in the world. We must all understand why William Tyndale chose the words he used in writing passages of scripture containing the word ἐκκλησία in Greek, and ekklesia when spoken in English! Let me say this a different way. **Jesus never made an error or mistake in the use of any word which He chose to give us to read**. Why would you now believe this? You perhaps might be correct in your assessment and with some reason caused by my statement, "How can you believe that?" Upon hearing this from you, I would be very inclined to say, "How can you not say this, or not believe it?" I would add with vigor, the following. Are you saying that our Lord Jesus could have made a mistake? No, surely not! Our Jesus, Our Savior, provided to us by our Heavenly Father, could and would use any word that He wanted to, because God made this provision for Him, enabling Him to say anything that He believed He should say! Do you not believe what you just read? Jesus knows any word that we might say, before we say it. If you, the reader, do not believe these short statements that reflect the Truth about our Savior, it will be impossible to please God, Christ Jesus, and the Holy Spirit. A Faith in God for mankind most certainly depends upon our abilities as His children, to give His son and our Savior an attitude of knowing what and how to say it, regardless of what it might be! Thank you readers, and I trust my statements never offend anyone unless they be given to me from within the Bible by My God and/or His appointed Helpers in Heaven and/or on earth.

So How, And When, Will You And I, Do What We Can, To Get Those We Know, Ourselves, And As Many Others As Possible, To At Least, Give Some Genuine Thought To This Problem!--That Is: How Can We Become Members Of A Congregacion Or An Assembly of Christ?

It is time to admit that we (you, I, and all who meet as Christians) don't have all the answers! At the same time, it is up to us and those who call themselves Christians to design a way to get there from here! Perhaps you have had trouble digesting what you have been reading. You may be saying, "I can't take anymore," yet we must continue to ask ourselves, "How much did **Jesus** take for all?" **He** gave His all, for All of us! He is trying to give us **Faith, Holiness,** and **Love**, the ingredients of Eternity with **Him**, **His Father**, and the **Holy Spirit. Admitting We Have A Problem? Yes!**

Once you and I admit that we have a problem, we should develop what might be a resolution to that which is bothering us! Let's begin to list those items that may strike us as being problems and list at the same time, possible solutions to those problems. Jesus had already said what He wanted and how to make it happen! **Matt. 16:18, Jesus said, "I will build My ἐκκλησία... That is, Congregacion"** It appeared in Koine Greek as Ekklesia, the Old English translation as it appears in the English language. William Tyndale did this marvelous work of translation of the New Testament Bible in A.D. 1525-26. Tyndale knew English and seven other languages, yet the unexpected by men, did happen in A.D. 1611. Out came a Bible referred to as the King James Bible, Authorized Version. **In today's world, Congregacion would be spelled Congregation and Assembly would continue to be spelled the same way as yesteryear!**

You and I know that it was translated incorrectly in several places, when at the King's direction, his translators did as he commanded them. Most obvious to bible scholars was the translation of the word in Koine Greek. In English it looked like this and was pronounced as Ekklesia. This word gave rise to two words meaning the same thing:

Congregacion and/or Assembly. King James 1st wanted and received the word **church** as a result of his power to do so. You will recall that this word in question was indeed **church** and was not used by Jesus, nor was He the author of that word, even though the world applauds this action as though it was coated by gold.

I wonder …. Do you think that the King read from his new version of the Bible, the King James Bible, Authorized Version, A.D. 1611? I wonder just how proud he was of himself. I also wonder if the King read from the book which was translated enough in his time to get a good long look at Galatians 1: 6-9.

Perversion of the Gospel: Read Gal. 1:6-9

From the Amplified Bible, Galatians 1:6-9

The Apostle Paul wrote these verses between A.D. 48-57

v6 "I am surprised and astonished that you are so quickly turning renegade and deserting Him Who invited and called you by the Grace (unmerited favor of Christ, The Messiah) [and that you are transferring your allegiance] to a different [even an opposition gospel]. v7 which is really not another [genuine gospel], but there are obviously some [people masquerading as teachers] who are distributing and confusing [with a misleading, counterfeit teaching] and want to distort the gospel of Christ twisting it into something which it absolutely is not]. v8 But even if we, or an angel from heaven, should preach to you a gospel contrary to that which we originally preached to you, let him be accursed (anathema, devoted to destruction, doomed to eternal punishment)! v9 As we said before, so I now say again: If anyone is preaching to you a gospel different from or contrary to that which you received [from us], let him be accursed (anathema' devoted to destruction, doomed to eternal punishment)!" The words of life were and still are true faith in Christ and His message of Salvation. If per chance you have a New Testament called **New Amplified Bible,** you might enjoy reading from that Bible from the **Lockman Foundation, La Habra, Ca. 90631 Copyright, 2015. My Current Bible is from this company, and I now write from this Bible today published in 1987.**

Revelation 22:18-19, Amplified Bible: A revelation by Jesus, written by the Apostle John. v18 "I testify and warn everyone who hears the words of the prophecy of this book [its predictions, consolations, and admonitions]: if anyone

adds [anything] to them, God will add to him the plagues (afflictions, calamities) which are written in this book, v19 and if anyone takes away from or distorts the words of the book of this prophecy, God will take away [from that one] his share from the tree of life and from the holy City (new Jerusalem), which are written in this book." **Solutions To Follow God's Will.**

What is the best way to honor Jesus' request? After all, He gave His life! Here is one idea. Within the last few years, I used the example below at least three times while I gave the communion thoughts to our congregation. This occurred without mentioning the word **church**. To not have done so, would to me have been an error of judgment. You may ask, "Why would you take such a step?" Until you take that first small step, you will not entertain larger and larger means of honoring God by changing from saying **church** (since it is not really something that Jesus requested), to using Jesus' preference of words like ekklesia, in English, and ἐκκλησία, or Assembly in Greek. Please permit me to read from the document below that I had used before the congregation, to be sure, that my mind would stay on track and not wander in my remarks, as is often the case with men who have attained that great old birthday numbered 84.

The Lord's Supper - Gateway Congregation of Christ - 10/10/16

Good Morning: We meet together this morning as Brothers and Sisters in Christ, in this congregation of Christians and others. This includes those of you who are traveling and are joining us to worship our Father, His Son and our Savior, Jesus Christ, and we have the presence of the Holy Spirit. If you are visiting with us, we invite you to partake of this Lord's Supper with those regularly assembled here today. And we invite you back as often as you can attend. I would like to read a paragraph of two sentences of what God expects of us as we prepare ourselves together to partake in this Communion Feast on this First day of the Week. This paragraph reads, "**After a person has left the world of Darkness and entered the Kingdom of God's dear Son with all its glorious light, he/she is to act in a completely different manner. The former acts are to be left behind; a whole new life should begin and continue until death or the second coming of Christ.**"

This brief paragraph was written by Dr. Stephen Eckstein, Jr., 97 years young, still going strong, with a mind as sharp as the proverbial Tack. His wife, Mildred, and he are living in Lubbock, Texas.

We know well that this memorial supper, which we are about to partake, was inaugurated by Jesus on the night of His betrayal by Judas, one of His own (**Matt. 26:26-28**). It is to be observed by Christians in memory of the Lord's death (**1ˢᵗ Cor. 11:24-25**). The emblems--unleavened bread and fruit of the vine--are used in this, our fellowship this day, and for every first day of the week. In this communion together, we symbolize the Lord's Supper, each of us personally, remembering the body and blood of Jesus, **1ˢᵗ Cor. 10:16**. "And upon the first day of the week, the disciples came together to break bread." (**Acts 20:7**) God has given us another First Day! Let us Pray.

Prayer for Bread: Father in Heaven, We are so grateful to be called a Congregation or an Assembly of Christians. We desire to continue to do work in your name. We thank you for your Son, Jesus, who died upon the cross to provide us a great opportunity to spend Eternity with all the Saints who will be a part of the Eternal **congregation**! Give us the words we need so often to invite others to learn of You and Your Son, the Messiah, whose Body upon the cross is now remembered, by unleavened bread. Accept our thanks! It is in His name we pray! Amen.

Prayer for Fruit of the Vine: Dear God, Thank You for this meaningful and beautiful Day of Remembrance! We know that you created us and have given to us a blessing of life, not only presently, but life everlasting. Continue to cleanse our hearts Dear God, and help us leave behind us, no desire for sin. Help us, God, as we begin to live forever and ever with You and Jesus Christ our Lord and the Holy Spirit, all along with our fellow Christians. In the memory of Jesus Christ, with this fruit of the vine which represents His blood shed for us, we dedicate our lives anew to Him and Trust Him completely! In His name we pray! Amen.

Time and Prayer for Giving: (Now is the time to use this space between the Lord's Supper and the Sermon of the Day for remembering in prayer, those who may be needy and/or sick or other.) **Our Father in Heaven:** Once again we come before you Lord, at this special time with gifts of money and the wishing of your healing powers on those with us this morning who are in need of prayer and your Blessings of Life. May our money and/or gifts be used wisely by our leadership in this congregation to assist those visitors or others among us in dire need of help in his or her household. In the name of our Lord Jesus we pray, Amen

Other Possibilities

Comparing different types of words in use in a **congregation**, reflecting on the word **church**, and many other wordlike ideas, we may be able to help solve our problem, and if not solve it, at least expose it to the World. The question is, do Christian People have the courage as well as the time to help bring a solution to a problem of this magnitude? I can certainly understand one's hesitancy to become involved. This kind of involvement may have to be delayed until more people come to God for energy and more purposeful direction toward Faith. Time is perhaps slipping by faster than we can imagine. That is to say that when one is involved in making a living, the kind of productive time needed may not be available. This is certainly not a criticism; it is only a statement of truth. The following words (sentences) immediately below, come directly from the translation of the earliest pages of scripture. We see **one of the messages of Jesus, and the Apostles** who greatly served Him as builder of Faith, **that does not have the word church attached to it.** Yet, in the other version, of the same verse, **with no mention of the word church in it.** I know firsthand how this may temporarily hurt. For the first time in our lives, no doubt, we read pages of scripture from the new Testament with no mention of the word **church**. Let's examine some of the written words as spoken by Christ in or around A.D. 31-33 that did make it into the Good Book that contains the only real and complete truth to a New Testament Christian!

Col. 4:15 The author is **William Tyndale in A.D. 1525-26.** The language is in Koine Greek, and he has the task of translating this Greek into Old English. The translation reads: **"Salute the brethren which are in Laodicea and salute the congregacion which is in his housse."** Notice the word Church does not appear. Why? Because Tyndale knew what Jesus wanted! He did not want a **church**, or he would have said so! He wanted a **Congregacion and/or Assembly of Christians.**

Col. 4:15 This is the translation of the same passage of scripture as above, however it was translated in about A.D. 1611 **by the translators for King James 1st, KJB, Authorized Version. It reads as follows: "Salute the brethren which are in Laodicea and Nymphas, and the church which is in his house."** It is interesting to show how translators of Greek interpreted the message that Tyndale translated in A.D. 1525-26. After the theft of the word **church** by King James 1st in A.D. 1611, two Greek Scholars named Stephens and Elzevir had about the same style and technique in their writing and in the translation of words. Scholars were touched!

Indicated prior, they apparently wrote so much alike that the usual recognition they received was to place Stephens' name first and then place a capital E nearby, to indicate that the Greek translation by each was very similar in content. In essence, they were given the same thanks for work created that reflected the heart and soul of each of the translators. Now, please read the following scripture translated by Stephens and/or Elzevir, approximately 25-50 years apart from that of William Tyndale.

Acts 16:5 "The assemblies therefore were strengthened in the faith and abounded in number every day." Notice, they did not use the word church.

Are we impressed with two great scholars, great and knowledgeable about their work? I am greatly impressed, and I pray that you feel the same feeling I have when I compare the two works! I can hardly wait to write the same verse, and you and I will be able to differentiate the result from both translations.

Acts 16:5 "And so were the churches established in the faith and increased in number daily.

All I can say is it doesn't make sense to me! Why did the King have to steal great words from the pattern that Jesus Christ wanted? Those words were **Congregacion** and/or **Assembly.** Frankly, it makes me want to bow my head and weep!

Now, let's be somewhat constructive in reviewing and working with the verse, **Acts 16:5,** as we judge the same verse three times, asking ourselves which choice would Jesus have made relative to: What His wish was to have been? In other words, which of the three choices of the three directions would have been most wise and selected by Jesus our Lord.

1. A.D. 1525-26 Acts 16:5 (Translated by William Tyndale) "And so were the congregacions stabblished in the faythh and increased in noumbre dayle."

2. A.D. 1611 Acts 16-5 (Translators for King James 1st) "And so were the churches established and being made stronger in the faith and increased.

3. A.D. 1550-1624 Acts 16:5 (Translated by Stephens(E)) 1550 and/or Elzevir "Assemblies therefore were strengthened in the faith and abounded in number every day."

If I were selecting a passage today from (#1. #2. #3.) that would fit His words and/or thoughts, I would suggest that it be from Tyndale, #1. That would be Jesus' choice! That was Jesus' choice! First Choice #1.

Passage #2 would be my last, or 3rd choice in the group of the three. Jesus made many references to overlooking His commands about Obedience.

Finally, third place is taken so I would find it very easy to give second place to Stephens and Elzevir. **(1st Place Paul, Jesus -Tyndale) (2nd Place Stephens-(E)lzevir) (3rd Place (King James)!**

The Origin Of The Word "Church," by Andy Zoppelt

Part I: The Word that Changed The World

Andy Zoppelt is a writer that all should read. Among others, he has written an outstanding work above, entitled The Origin of the Word "Church," as listed. **Part I: The Word that changed the World** was included as a subtitle. It is found, and you will be able to easily find his publications on Google, etc. The next four points belong to Andy Zoppelt.

1. Archbishop Bancroft and Erasmu were the architects of King James Version translation; they were far from being committed saints. The translators were obligated to fit the translation with the Anglican agenda and beliefs without any conflict between church and state. Their interest was not in the Kingdom of God but an institutional system with its paid clergy. The early assembly of believers did not have a clergy distinct from the rest of the body. Clergy with titles and authority was foreign to the early disciples. It was the rise of the authoritarian clergy that needed a building to control the people both religiously and politically and together the people around the clergy. The Catholic Church and the Church of England, both used the word "Church" and its meaning as a building to hold the people in subjection to their control. Without a building, the clergy would have lost their power over the people. Even today, without a building, the clergy system would fail. This system of clergy/aity and the use of a building as we have come to know, an "institutional" church system. This system was totally foreign to the vocabulary and life of the disciples of Jesus.

2. To change the true meaning and function of the Greek word "ekklesia" to our English word "Church" strengthened the clergy system and their power over the people. The statement, "power corrupts and absolute power corrupts absolutely" has been the downfall and corruption of body ministry. The original intent was relational and not institutional. For in all the writings of the first and second century we do not find an "institutional" treatment of "ekklesia." (Ekklesia-English) (ἐκκλησία-Koine Greek). (Greek), not a Church! Ekklesia translates only to Congregation and/or Assembly. Tyndale

created problems early on in his translation of the scriptures into English. Tyndale, a man who was martyred for His Bible, used the word "Church" (churche) only twice, in Acts 14:13 and 19:37; and in both cases he understandingly understood Church as a building connected to idol-worship. Here are the places he used the word Church. It is in old English: Acts 14:13 "Then lupiters Preste which dwelt before their cite brought oxe and garlondes vnto the churche porche and wolde have done sacrifise with the people." Now here is an updating version of his translation to present: Acts 14:13 "Then Jupiter's Priest which dwelt before their city brought oxen and garlands into the church [pagan house of worship] porch and would have done sacrifice with the people." Here is the other verse in which he used the word Church: Acts 19:37 "For ye have brought hither these men whiche are neither robbers of churches [pagan houses of worship] nor yet despisers of your goddess." Updating Acts 19:37-38. "For you have brought these men to me which are nether robbers of churches nor yet despisers of your goddess." The reference is to the temple and goddess of Diana of the Ephesians. A building would more serve the purpose of a religious group with a built- in hierarchy than an organic body of believers ministering and loving one another. Christians originally didn't build buildings for some kind of service as we see today. They were clearly distinguished from the pagans whose focus was on buildings, statues, ritual and physical objects. From its earliest usage, the word "Church" has been understood in pagan traditions, then later in Roman Catholicism and now in this present day, as a building, but never has the word "Church" been demonstrated or justified from a biblical standpoint to represent the Greek word ekklesia. What are we thinking when we read the Lord's prayer? "Your kingdom come, your will be done **on earth as it is in Heaven**...for yours is the kingdom, the power, and the glory." All what we see representative of the church today is against all that is representative of the kingdom of heaven.

3. Andy Zoppelt is quick and correct to say that Language and its use of words is vital, it is the fundamental means in which we use to convey and pass information from one person to another. The changing of one word can literally change the world.

Therefore, translators are given an extreme responsibility in making sure that they get it right, especially key words. When Jesus said, "Upon this rock I will build my ekklesia." (Matt. 16:18) The Greek word there is ekklesia and is pronounced ek-klay-see-ah. The translators purposely and knowingly used a word identifying a building to support a clergy rather than a word that would build us together as the body of Christ in unity establishing the Kingdom of God in every city. Jesus did not and would not have said, "upon this rock I will build my church." The word "Church" represents the complete opposite of building His Kingdom on this earth as it is in Heaven. Jesus would rather have said, "Upon this rock I will build my called out assembly," a people called out of this world by faith in Him, assembling and gathering in one name and for one purpose, all being one.

Our word "Church" is one of those words that has impacted the world and has subverted the whole purpose for which it was intended. Because the translators used the word "Church," meaning a building, instead of a more accurate word reflecting a functioning body, it has affected our **whole** approach to the meaning of the body of Christ. We have been given a word from the translators that has nothing to do with the original Greek word ekklesia. There is not a single Greek word to back up the whole church.

4. Zoppelt calls a tie of **equalization of power** between the **church and state, wrong, and suggests that this statement of "power corrupts and absolute power corrupts absolutely" has been the downfall and corruption of body ministry.** Zoppelt then continues with his comments. The framers of our constitution indeed understood the power of such a tie. But what we have today is a bunch of buildings called Church, with each pastor having his own Kingdom separated from others in the city... they guard that position and place with their lives. Our assemblies were never to be separated within the city... It was clearly one called out assembly in each city, as we see in scripture. Kingdoms are made up of cities within the Kingdom and that is what we see in scriptures with the assemblies in the city. The called out assemblies jointly made up the Kingdom of God with one King. It was the assembly at Ephesus, the assembly at Corinth and the assembly at Philadelphia, etc. There were not a bunch of churches ruled by pastors and elders in each city, that would constitute a division within the body of Christ and nullify His rule over the city assemblies... truly a gross injustice and sin.

This concludes my handling of the work from Andy Zoppelt and I again thank him for his great contribution to this book.

Let's squarely face the problem that many of us may be thinking is a real problem, when perhaps we are already facing the problem, if we are indeed believers. The problem becomes easy to solve. We simply must not rely on the **church** to save us, for we know that Jesus Christ, His Father, God and the Holy Spirit, without question, will save us. We cannot now and never should have relied on the **church** to save anyone! Why? and How? **Why, because following scripture is the right thing to do.** How? Even more simply stated! **If we are truly baptized, accept God's Grace, thus becoming a Christian and proceed to begin to welcome one another to worship within a Congregacion and/or an Assembly, we have very little to worry about, a joy-filled life ahead of us and an**

eternal home in heaven! Now, this being the opportunity that it is, we can start showing our fellow Christians more love, more attention, providing more help to meet their needs in our **Congregations** and/or **Assemblies**. We can begin to address Christianity as God says! Wait a minute! Did you not understand? What do you and I believe we need to do to address Christianity? Let's try this question. What do you think that we should be called? When we were baptized into the Father, Jesus Christ, and the Holy Spirit, we were called Christians. Christians were first called this name in Antioch. Do you recall that this was a long time before we ever encountered the incidents connected with King James 1st? Perhaps we need to read more scripture about baptism. What is really said as read directly from the Bible. Don't rely on a person to read the following scripture if you're in a position to examine it with them. If there is a medical or some other reading problem, then by all means, read it and explain it to him/her. Take the time now, if you will please, and become fully enamored with the flow of words when baptism is the main subject. You will read the following scriptures and I simply ask you to think what the scripture is saying about this viable instruction from our God-Christ-and-the-Holy-Spirit! Read: **Matt. 28:17-20 "And when they saw Him, they worshiped Him; but some doubted [that it was He] v18 Jesus came up and said to them, all authority (all power of absolute rule) in and on earth has been given to me. v19 Go therefore and make disciples of all the nations [help the people to learn of me, believe in Me, obey My words], baptizing them in the name of the Father and of the Son and of the Holy Spirit, v20 teaching them to observe everything that I have commanded you; and lo, I am with you always [remaining with you perpetually, regardless of circumstance, and one very occasion] even to the end of the age."** From the Amplified Bible (AMP) Copyright 2015, The Lockman Foundation, La Habra, CA

And now a very serious and inward look at the real you and me! We have the great benefit of the Story of Jesus. I am very happy to say this for those of us who have been baptized for the forgiveness of sins, accepted God's Grace and want to continue to follow the commands of Jesus for worthy living, while remaining the same Christian that we were before we ever read this book or a similar book that exposed us to the truth of God, Jesus, and the Holy Spirit. If and when we finally believe that we and millions of others have read the scripture, have obeyed Christ in Baptism, have obeyed and continue to obey the Commandments set forth by God, Jesus, and the Holy Spirit, (The Trinity) will be our every step to remain the Christian that we are now and the Christian trying more times than ever to be like They, the Trinity.

And if we are able to establish a continuing relationship with them by strongly identifying and working to seek others for Christ and are continuing to live the Life that the Powers of Heaven want us to live, we can reestablish the fact that we continue to Live for Jesus. **I, for example, am a Member of the Gateway Congregation of Christ that meet in the City of Ruidoso, New Mexico!** What I am trying to say in a very gentle way is, Don't hold to any truth, until or unless, **you prove absolutely to yourself that you have the truth, that will cause or already has caused the God-Head above to reserve a place for you in Eternity.**

My desire is to show you in the entirety of this reading, in this book, what members of the Churches of Christ and other denominations can easily adapt to, as more and more we lose the word **church** (hopefully) from all manuscripts called Bibles. This is due, of course to its wrong placement in the Bible. William Tyndale had correctly translated exactly what had been translated as a word of God, from our Messiah and our Lord Jesus Christ. Jesus did **NOT** use the word **church** to address the English translation of the Koine Greek that He spoke. Instead, beginning with King James 1st and several religious leaders craving more than truth, such as money and power, the words that Tyndale had used because Jesus spoke those words, had been changed to **church** to bring a type of religion that would keep the forces in power over the people, so long as the civilization could succeed in what it was doing. Unfortunately, there is no warranty, except true Believers, that guarantee an Eternity in Heaven with God, Christ, and the Holy Spirit. Those people who believed the truth and became (immersed believers) honored the direction as provided, that being the commandments of God and living as specified in continuing obedience.

King James 1st and his cohorts brought about and used the word **church**, yet Jesus had said long before King James came into the picture that He would use, and did so in practice, the words that came from His own language, Ekklesia in English from Koine Greek, for two words that translated directly from (ἐκκλησία-Koine Greek) known as **Congregation and/or Assembly!** In Chapter One of this book, while observing the early writings of William Tyndale, you saw the number of times (115) that the word **church was absolutely silent and deliberately so at the direction of our Savior, Jesus the Messiah**. And you recall in this chapter, you observed the writings of Andy Zoppelt, who showed us the use of the word church **two times, as used in the Book of Acts.** Each use was to show that the word **church was a word connected with a term spelled out as pagan house of worship. Yes, and I also recall the terminology which fit the situation, that being, a building connected to Idol Worship.** Need I say any more?

I repeat, I am a Member of the Gateway Congregation of Christ in Ruidoso, New Mexico who meet faithfully on each Lord's Day and at other times at the direction/invitation of the elders and/or minister. Even at Gateway there are some whose passion is a **church**. In my opinion, this has really put an obstacle in the way of full membership for that Body of Christ.

Had we only been a part of this original gathering! What we have done is to find ourselves separate and apart, knowing what should have been done, yet realizing that the **church** stands squarely in the way. I never would have dreamed that this wording would have come from me. Here is (my/our) problem. When King James 1st got his way, he stepped in our way. When the King got his **church**, and make no doubt about it, it was a **church**, an automatic barrier was set in action. So, I ask Why? Why did all of this occur? And you know what? I think I have an answer. Notice, I did not say I had The answer! The answer must come from you and I and from as many Biblically oriented people as we are able to gather together and Worship our King as He wanted! Yes, had I really known, perhaps I could have stopped when I got the feeling that this was something bigger than I, and I need assistance. (Yet I was multi years late!)

But you know, I am not getting a lot of help to rectify the situation. And perhaps if I were an onlooker, I would say the same things. Thanks, but no thanks! Those who try to do something when they are certain that something needs to be done, may not have time left to do anything that adds to the list of things to be done!

Chapter Three

Are You Prepared To Meet God, Christ, and the Holy Spirit?

The Coming of Eternal Life

In **Gen. 15:6** (AMP Bible) we read, "**And he [Abram] believed in, (trusted in, relied-on, remained steadfast to) the Lord and He counted it to him as righteousness (right standing with God).**" Please also see **Rom. 4:3 and Gal. 3:6**

Gen. 17:6 records God's word to Abraham, stating, "**And I will make you exceedingly fruitful and I will make nations of you, Kings will come from you.**" Abraham is in the lineage of us all and first, the father of the 12 tribes of Israel. Thus, in the period that we refer to as the Patriarchal Age, God for the most part communicated directly **with His chosen people. God counted the Faith and Obedience of Abraham as Righteous---Right Standing with God**.

There is an apparent concept, often not so visible or transparent, that may be stated as follows: If one stands for what he or she believes is the truth, it will be necessary to examine and reexamine that body of truth, as we stand to be counted by God, as God's people, as members of Christ's Body, as baptized believers, in the process of being built as a part of the congregations that Jesus said He would build, and in the process of being made completely and fully right in God's sight. Therefore, an individual who through Faith and Obedience has become a part of the building process, a part of the congregations and or assemblies, has now become a citizen in the Kingdom of Heaven. This Kingdom is a temporal Kingdom, and when we are completed as a product of the Spiritual building process, by Christ, here on earth, upon our death we will be transferred into the Eternal Kingdom of God, Christ, and the Holy Spirit. Additionally, we shall enjoy the people with us since the beginning of time, as judged by Jesus Christ our Savior, and His Father, God. I would also believe that we will renew our ties with the Holy Spirit. In **2nd Peter 1:11**, we read: "**Thus, there will be richly and abundantly provided for you your entry into the eternal Kingdom of our Lord and Savior Jesus Christ.**" (Amp. Version)

The Eternal Kingdom of our Lord and Savior is as it says, eternal. Once we receive entrance into this Kingdom upon Christ's return, we will be with the God-Head, including the Holy Spirit and the Chosen People throughout the Ages, from the Beginning of Time to the End of Time, as man counts time! But God does not count that way and we will rapidly understand what the term eternity includes, on God's term! So, with whom will we spend eternity? The answer: Followers of the Gospel of Christ, from the Beginning of Time. One part would seem to be: Men and Women of Old--The Patriarchal Age, made Righteous in the sight of God. Strong Faith and Obedience to His will is an answer. It would include Noah, Abraham, Isaac, and their offspring, the beginning of the twelve tribes and many others. Not one could earn his/her salvation. Generally speaking, this would be from Moses to Christ, the latter being the only one who was able to keep the law. Those who had a strong Faith and obeyed God were counted as Righteous (were in Right Standing with God). Not one could earn his/her salvation! These people of God, Christ, and the Holy Spirit were very familiar with the word, ekklesia! He said He would build His ekklesia and that includes all, who through a strong Faith, are obeying God's and Christ's Will.

These structures are now in progress of being built. We are Spiritual citizens of the Kingdom of Heaven, abiding here on earth and this can be better understood, in my opinion, if we say that the ekklesia--**Congregations** and/or **Assemblies** that He is building have a place in the sovereign Kingdom of Heaven, His Headquarters! See **1st Peter 3:22**, from the Amplified Bible. **"[And He] has now entered into Heaven and is at the right hand of God, with [all] angels and authorities and powers made subservient to Him."**

Who else will be in heaven? Anyone who the God-Head sees fit to save. God is, and He can do anything that He pleases. It seems to me that we have plenty to fill our plate without giving much discussion to this issue, particularly at this time. However, I can think of one great beneficial point that can be made by studying God's decision to act in certain ways! That point very simply is "Fear God and Keep His Commandments." We pray that we, our families and our friends will be with us!

Jesus said He would build His **Ekklesia:** In Koine Greek this word, as you well know by now, looks like this, ἐκκλησία, and is pronounced as ek-klay-see-ah. For without a good understanding of ekklesia, the congregation as a part of any culture cannot be properly placed as a part of our mindset. By now, I hope the next paragraph somewhat shocks you! If only the word **church** had not been used!

It is important to quickly look with some insight and analysis into what we in the past have referred to as the **church**. About 56 years ago, I recall reading a book by a brother J. Riddly Stroop[1], an elder in a congregation as noted below in the footnote. The title of

---

[1] (First Edition: This Is God's World: Listen As He Speaks To Us, pp. 36,37 - Published by Xulon Press, 2015, Dr. Roger L. Harrell)

the book was the Church of the Bible. The concept of the ekklesia is very important. Members of the ekklesia, the Body of Christ, are sometimes confused by translations. In fact, it seems to me most of the world is confounded by Biblical translations!

I readily admit that I was one of them. I was introduced to this in the small community of McAlister, New Mexico about 72 years ago, and was around 12 years of age. Most all of the families had King James Bibles. It was King James or keep your thoughts to yourself! At that point, I must admit that on a farm far away from a city, I could not spend much time observing what everyone else might have been looking at, that being a brand new King James Bible, Authorized Version. If you had one of those, man did you have money! It was an adult class, but above 12 years of age you were pretty much an adult. (Not really, but we thought so!)

The class on that Lord's Day was about **Acts Chapter 7 and verse 38.** And for everyone's benefit, I will print the 38th verse from the 7th Chapter for our reading, and for your information the date of printing of this Bible was stamped in the appropriate place. I will be reading from a first printing produced by Zondervan in 1958. (**v38 "This was he, that was in the church in the wilderness with the angel which spake to him in the mount Sinai, and with our fathers: who received the lively oracles to give unto us."**)

Now permit me to have just a bit of fun. The next paragraph was typed by William Tyndale who was responsible to put in print, his original, Edition Number One. This would have been done in A.D. 1525-26. This was the original script from Tyndale, and for many years (about 86 yrs.) was the protocol for the way that Jesus had given authority to do so, that practically everyone used in this time period. Recall its demise by King James 1st, A.D. 1611.

Acts 7:38 Original writings by William Tyndale, A.D. 1525-26. "This is he that was in ye congregacion in the wyldernes with the angell which spake to him in ye moute Syna and with oure fathers. This man receave the worde of lyfe to geve vnto."

So Much Difference! So Much Change from Tyndale to King James! Who would ever believe it?

How many of you presently reading this book are still in disbelief? How many of you may be, still yelling at me silently? I apologize, but I believed that it was the only right thing to do. It is time for us to re-adapt! But it is very difficult to do. For a while, no one will believe you or me. You may even see a friend and he/she will look away! Not a pleasant sight! However, it is time to return to the story that took place in McAlister, New Mexico, when I was about 12 years old. **The Sunday School teacher had just decided to ask his question!**

It was fresh on everyone's mind and the gentleman was really charged up. Then out of his mouth in a louder than usual voice came a resounding question! **"Brothers and sisters," he said, "what is the meaning of this question?"** The brother quickly responded, **"It means exactly what it says. It was the Church of Christ in the Wilderness."** Then, the brother had a strange look on his face. His eyes were rolling up and down. He thought quietly to himself, "This is not the **church** that Jesus said He would build." No one really had a sound answer. In fact, there was not a sound! Maybe it is a misprint? No one believed that! This was a tough time in **church** (sarcasm) at McAlister, New Mexico. Ten to twelve years later, I came across Brother Stroop's book, **The Church of the Bible.** It was strange, very strange reading at first. As I read it, I could not believe it. It was somewhat frightening to read what Brother Stroop had written. It was a fresh and interesting approach. But it did not sound like the Church of Christ that I had known for many years. Let me share with you the mystery that unfolded as I read and reread this material. I almost feel that this was a miracle in my life! But it took a long time to awaken this miracle.

More On The ἐκκλησία

One of the last things I learned from my additional studies in this book, was that the word **church** does not actually appear in the Bible, at least not as a building, or housing and/or hiring unknown people and attaching them somehow to God. However, time and time again, you will get the picture that solidifies Jesus Christ as our Lord and Savior. For example, most of the English speaking were the first to call the structure where we worship Christ, a **church**. But that was not correct according to Tyndale and Jesus.

I taught a lesson to the members of the Church of Christ while working in Carlsbad, New Mexico about 35 years ago. At that time, I was the Superintendent of Schools. I will never forget the look on the face of one of the elders when I said, **"The word church, as we use it, is not even in the Bible."** And technically, that is a correct statement! That was the good news! The bad news was this was the last time I was asked to teach anything in Carlsbad that had to do with the Bible and religion. There is no direct translation from the Koine Greek word for **church**, lest it be about a couple of thousand years before Christ was born to this earth for very special reasons of beginning his initial stay in Heaven with His Father.

ἐκκλησία means an **Assembly** or **Congregation** of God's people, who have been baptized into Christ, our redeemer and Savior. Instead of Church of Christ, Jesus said He would build His ἐκκλησία -ekklesia. I have established and verified in print with notations, throughout this book, that the word for ekklesia (ἐκκλησία) may be translated from Koine Greek to one of two words in English and the words are **Congregation and/or Assembly**. William Tyndale, who was the most famous and deliberate thinker, and the one who received the translation of Koine Greek so as to pull the words of Christ from death to life, knew what the task was and what he needed to do. Tyndale, as opposed to King James 1st, was the first to understand what was happening; therefore, he wrote what he needed to write to do what Jesus wanted him to do. When the translators thought that the group meetings had no "religious connotation," the word ekklesia was translated assembly. This is extremely significant for us as we strive to better understand the Will of God. Had Jesus wanted to build a **church** that came with power and defined as the Lord's House, He would have used the Greek word Kuriakon, derived from the word Kurios, meaning Lord or Master. Kuriakon denotes a Body Politic, an organization with power-centered leaders. Jesus simply wanted to build ἐκκλησίας, **Assemblies and/or Congregations** of Believers, designated as God's people, Christians, as per the Great Design of God and Christ. Yes, Jesus Himself gave an accountable abundance to the world through His Death--Burial--Resurrection and His Ascension back to God.

I close this chapter with a few quotes from Riddly Stroop. According to Stroop in the **Church of the Bible, "the word Kingdom designates a type of relationship which demands the recognition of authority and provides assurances to those who give it. This is the case of Christian Relationship. A Person accepts Jesus as Lord, Ruler, and King, following His teaching implicitly, and looking to Him for the blessings that have been promised!"** Stroop had information that all of us should have about the **Church**! See below.

"On the other hand, the word church makes no direct reference to man's vital relationship with God, but rather has exalted the human side of Christianity and attributed to the church, privileges and powers which have never been granted to it and which practice has blinded people to the Gospel of Christ, leading them to put their faith in the church and not in Christ and to comply with the teaching of the church of which they are members rather than the teaching of Christ." Again, here is Riddly Stroop: **"The Gospel that was preached in the first century was the Gospel of the Kingdom not the Gospel of the church. The Mysteries that were made known to the apostles, and through them to others, were the mysteries of the King."**

Chapter Four

A Pathway That Discloses An Acceptable Conscience To Eternal Life

One can readily tell that the writer of this book favors a Bible named the **Amplified Bible**. I hesitate to name favorites, but it follows a pattern that seems to make my job responsibility more information-directed toward the subject, and it explains the verses so well to the readers. When you have read this short chapter, I trust that you will agree. My comments will be less than few, namely only those that I am now writing. The journey toward Heaven requires a Clean and Acceptable Conscience that directs the pathway. Please relax and enjoy these most worthy words that have been recorded from our Father and his Son, our Savior, Jesus Christ in the sacred pages of our Bible.

1.   **Hebrews 9:8-10** "By this the Holy Spirit signifies that the way into the Holy Place [the true Holy of Holies and the presence of God] has not yet been disclosed[2] as long as the first or outer tabernacle is still standing, [that is, as long as the Levitical system of worship remains a recognized institution], **v9** for this [first or outer tabernacle] is a symbol [that is, an archetype or paradigm] for the present time. Accordingly, both gifts and sacrifices are offered which are incapable of perfecting the conscience and renewing the [inner self of the] worshiper. **v10** For they [the gifts, sacrifices and ceremonies] deal only with [clean and unclean] food and drink and various ritual washings, [mere] external regulations for the body imposed [to help the worshipers] until the time of reformation [that is, the time of the new order when Christ will establish the reality of what these things foreshadow, a better covenant.]"

2.   **1st Peter 3:20-22** "who once were disobedient, when the great patience of God was waiting in the days of Noah, during the building of the ark, in which a few, that is, eight persons [Noah's Family], were brought safely through the water. **v21** Corresponding to that [rescue through the flood], baptism [which is an expression of a believer's new life in Christ] now saves[3] you, not by removing dirt from the body, but by an appeal to God for a (good clear) conscience [demonstrating what you believe to be yours] through the resurrection of Jesus Christ, **v22** who has gone into heaven and is at the right hand of God [that is, the place of honor and authority], with [all] angels and authorities and powers made subservient to Him."

3.   **Acts 2:34-35** "For David did not ascend into the heavens; yet, he himself says, The

---

[2] **Heb. 9:8** During the age of the old covenant a worshiper had no direct access to God.
[3] **1st Peter 3:21** Baptism is a public representation of that which actually saves the believer--one's personal faith in death, burial and resurrection of Jesus the Messiah.

Lord said to my Lord, Sit at My right hand and share My throne **v35** Until I make Your enemies a footstool for your feet."

4.	**1st Cor. 15:22-28** " For just as [because of their union of nature] in Adam **all** people die, so also by [virtue of their union of nature] shall all **in Christ** be made alive. **v23** But each in his own rank and turn: Christ (the Messiah) (is) the first fruits, then those who are Christ's [own will be resurrected] at His coming. **v24** After that comes the end (the completion), when He delivers over the kingdom to God the Father after rendering inoperative and abolishing every [other] rule and every authority and power. **v25** For [Christ] must be King and reign until He has put all [His] enemies under His feet. **v26** The last enemy to be subdued and abolished is death. **v27** For He [the Father] has put all things in subjection under His [Christ's] feet. But when it says, All things are put in subjection [under Him], it is evident that He [Himself] is excepted Who does the subjecting of all things to Him. **v28** However, when everything is subjected to Him, then the Son Himself will also subject Himself to [the Father] Who put all things under Him, so that God may be all in all [be everything to everyone, supreme, the indwelling and controlling factor of life]."

5.	**2nd Peter 1:11** "Thus there will be richly and abundantly provided for your entry for you in the eternal kingdom of our Lord and Savior Jesus Christ."

6.	**Hebrews 12:1-2** "Therefore then, since, we are surrounded by so great a cloud of witnesses [who have borne testimony to the Truth], let us strip off and throw aside every encumbrance (unnecessary weight) and that sin which so readily (deftly and cleverly) clings to and entangles us, and let us run patient endurance and steady and active persistence the appointed course of the race that is set before us. **v2** Looking away [from all that will distract] to Jesus, Who is the Leader and the Source of our faith [giving the first incentive for our belief] and is also its Finisher [bringing it to maturity and perfection]. He for the joy [of obtaining the prize] that was set before Him, endured the cross, despising and ignoring the shame, and is now seated at the right hand of the throne of God."

7.	**Hebrews 12:23-29** "And to the congregation of the Firstborn who are registered [as citizens] in heaven, and go to the God who is Judge of all, and to the spirits of the religious (the redeemed in heaven) who have been made perfect, **v24** And to Jesus the Mediator (Go-between, Agent) of a new covenant, and to the sprinkled blood which speaks [of mercy], a better and nobler and more gracious message than the blood of Abel [which cried out for vengeance]. **v25** So see to it that you do not reject Him or refuse to listen to and heed Him Who is speaking [to you now]. For if they [the Israelites] did not escape when they refused to listen and heed Him Who warned and divinely instructed them [here] on earth [revealing with heavenly warnings His will], how much less shall we escape if we reject and turn our backs on Him who cautions and admonishes [us] from heaven? **(26)** Then [at Mount Sinai] His voice shook the earth, but now He has given a promise: Yet once more I will shake and make tremble not only the earth but also the [starry] heavens. **v27** Now this expression, Yet, once more, indicates the final removal and transformation of all [that can be] shaken--that is, of that which has been created--in order that what cannot be shaken may remain and continue. **v28** Let us therefore, receiving a kingdom that is firm and stable and cannot be shaken, offer to God pleasing service and acceptable worship, with modesty and pious care and godly fear and awe; **v29** For our God [is indeed] a consuming fire."

Chapter Five

Living a life of Righteousness

Appropriating God's Grace--Is There A Difference?

When I heard this question, it sounded puzzling! It took a while. This was talk of two different things as though they were one and the same. But they were not! What? Are you sure? I hope to give you, the reader, much more information than I received on that one night. Tell us about that night! Well, we had the advantage of a smaller congregation out in the country, with what I thought to be, excellent discussions coming from a variety of ministers and from want-to-be-ministers for the Body of Christ. They had enrolled in a school at Portales, New Mexico, to attend Eastern New Mexico University.

It was a one-way trip to McAlister, N.M. where they preached Sunday morning, spent the day with the farming residents, then on Sunday night of the same day, offered instruction to the farmers and their families. These services were held for the community of those who wanted to learn more about God, Christ, and the Holy Spirit. Now, about the **church**: you see, we had not heard anything about calling a **church**, anything but a **church**. And this building was a Church of Christ. It was located near the community grocery store, with available gasoline and food stuff. The only other building at the location and/or nearby, as just described, was a building that was named McAlister, New Mexico. In that building were groceries, soda pop, and a small post office. On the way home from schools out in the country, McAlister (Grade School) and House, New Mexico, (High School), the bus driver would always stop on the way to deliver us to our homes. He knew that each student on the bus, one with a small 20 seat capacity, would have about 20 cents; and he was right. The bus driver probably had about $3.00 and he was to bring some groceries home to his family after he took care of his bus route! Yes! Kids on the bus used the 20 cents for pop, candy, and chewing gum.

I believe it to be proper to use some notes that I took from the lips of most of the ministers that came to our location to preach the Gospel. These dusty notes extended way back to about 1959. Many of those men, if not all of them, have passed on to greater things to be with God, and Christ the King.

There is a scripture in the Old Testament that seems to take firm hold upon God Himself concerning Appropriating His Grace. Look at Psalms 119:57 "You are my portion, O Lord; I have promised to keep Your words." Here, it seems that the Psalmist takes firm hold upon God Himself, appropriating God's Grace. Is this true?

Grace Is The Unmerited Favor Of God Toward Mankind.

Perhaps the parable of the prodigal son is the most obvious example. In that parable, Grace is extended to one who seemingly has no basis on which to be shown Grace, other than the fact he has asked in humility and repentance to be shown it!

Law Was Given Through Moses, The Better Things Of Grace And Truth = Christ (John 1:17)

Chapter 20 of the Book of Exodus, beginning with verse one is a statement from God, which records a collection of things that God spoke to His People, that included things that they **should do and/or not do. Exodus 1:20** "Then God spoke all these words." It would do all of us well indeed if we would read Chapter one and two from this book on a regular basis. God says it like it is! He holds no punches and after reading we can ask ourselves, what have we done that He has told us not to do, or what did we do, which He told us to do.

Connecting Grace to Eternity

In connecting grace to election, Paul sees God as electing us before the creation of the world for the purpose of holiness and blamelessness (Eph. 1:4) He predestined us to be adopted as sons and daughters into the family of God. (Eph. 1:5) All of this elective work is so that we might "praise His glorious grace."

In other words, election and grace go hand in hand because of their free character. We can do nothing to deserve them! This preceding statement may be an overstatement as mankind views it. If we obey our Lord in baptism, that is to be completely immersed in water, as God, Christ, and the Holy Spirit have told us, is this not a way, perhaps the only way, to show our conviction that Jesus Christ is our personal Savior? Does not God reward us with salvation upon our request and thanks to Him for doing so and on evidence of obeying His word as He has commanded? What do we do to deserve such a thing?

This grace is therefore the hope that is stored up for us in return for complete obedience to Their Word, in Heaven. (Eph. 5:5) One force is the Grace of God. A second Force is our obedience to God for the promise of Eternal Life. Are these forces equal? What is in store for us if we do not obey our Lord? Let's read Eph. 1:7 It says, "In Him we have redemption (Deliverance and Salvation) through His blood, the remission (forgiveness) of our offenses (shortcomings and trespasses), in accordance with the riches and the generosity of His gracious Favor." What more could we ask for?

This Godly news which touches places that have no borders is to be found in Romans, the 3rd Chapter, verses 23-27.

Romans 3:23-27 states quite clearly that all have fallen short of the glory of God and are "justified freely by His grace through the redemption that came by Jesus Christ." Hence the unmerited favor of God buys us legal freedom from our sin and cancels the sentence of guilt the Judge has had to declare in order **v26** "to be just and the one who justified those who have faith in Jesus." It is interesting to note that the next thought of Paul is: "Where, then, is boasting? It is excluded."

We again, are emphasizing that Grace is free and God, not man, is in control. You, no doubt will be pressed by your own quest to read at least all of the Holy Writ encompassed in Romans, Chapters 3, 4, 5 and 6. It will be a blessing to you upon the culmination of this reading in the book and chapters cited!

In Eph. 2:8-9 Paul states the free character of grace perhaps even more explicitly, now, not using the language of justification, but simply of salvation. **We are told that we have been saved "by grace" but "through faith."** Grace is seen here as the means by which we are saved, a free gift. Faith is seen as the mechanism by which that salvation or grace is appropriated. Paul must then go on to argue that even faith is **v9** "not by works so that no one can boast."

Ephesians is a Golden Book of eternal life. I trust that you will want to stop reading at this point in my book and turn your attention to Chapters one through six in Ephesians. Read the entire letter written by Paul. It is Godly reading! The entire book will help us exercise the dimension that the Lord our God would like for us to read and digest.

In Romans 5:2, Paul speaks of gaining "access by faith into this grace in which we now stand" and in 5:21 of grace reigning "through righteousness to bring eternal life through Jesus Christ our Lord."

Even the suffering of the present Christian life is linked to the Grace that God gives us. In Paul's famous statement about the thorn in his flesh, 2nd Cor. 12:7-10, he speaks of asking three times that this thorn be taken from him, only to receive the answer, "**My Grace is sufficient for you, for My power is made perfect in weakness." Here, Grace is equated with the power to live the Christian life and to do ministry in the name of**

Christ. So Paul delights even in the hardships of that ministry. In a similar way, the whole of the Christian life is linked to Grace, as evidenced in Titus 2:11-14. This Grace **"teaches us to say no to ungodliness and worldly passions, and to live self-controlled, upright and Godly lives in this present age, while we wait for the blessed Hope."** One of the great Books of the Bible is the one in which Paul states we have different gifts, "according to the Grace given us." Read verses 3-8 in Romans, the 12th Chapter!

The notion of Grace as connected to the Spirit of God is continued by the author of Hebrews in such a way that even mentions "the Spirit of Grace" (Heb. 10:22-39). The sacred writings recorded in the Book of Hebrews also emphasize the connection of Grace to salvation (2:9), sanctification (4:16, 12:15, 13:9), and the final blessing of God (13:25). Now, let us travel over some of the ground we have covered in this short Chapter and see if indeed, we can make a general rule for differentiating between: **(A.) Appropriating Grace and (B.) Living a Life of Righteousness**

Tell me what you are reading as I am writing in the following sentence: **Grace is the unmerited favor of God toward mankind!** Are you saying that no one but Christ or God with the help and assurance of the Holy Spirit can become a beacon of light and salvation, instantaneously, for lost mankind? **Yes, how right you are!** Recall earlier in this chapter this quotation: In Eph. 2:8-9, Paul states the free character of grace perhaps even more explicitly, now not using the language of justification, but simply of salvation. **We are told that we have been saved "by grace," but "through faith." Grace is seen here as the means by which we are saved, a free gift. Faith is seen as the mechanism by which that salvation or grace is appropriated. Or must we recognize them equally strong at the same time?**

We are now at the crossroads **to say and to mean** that we are saved by two things: (1) **Faith,** to Christ and **God's demand of Obedience of Righteousness and the Commands of Christ** and by (2) **our Appropriation of His Grace!** I believe we are hearing a message that will keep us on the right track to Heaven. What comes to mind as the first indication that something big is about to happen? Do **we appropriate** the Grace that God has for us, or do we become mindful of the scripture that helps in every turn in the road to obey our Father and keep our Savior Jesus Christ by our side by doing what He is asking us to do? May I ask you a very personal question? Which do you think is the stronger of the two Keys to Eternity? **Your Faith in the God-Head or Your willingness to appropriate Grace from our God-Head? Have you ever thought anyone would ask you this question?**

Let me pose another question. Which do you perceive to be the strongest mechanism of obedience and Christian love to God? Christ and the Holy Spirit? Faith or Grace? Which comes first, Faith or Grace and Why? If you have no faith in God, why would you worry about securing God's Grace? If you have Strong and **Living Faith in Christ,** why would you **wait even one minute** to ask for **Grace** from our Father in Heaven? I see the God-Head keeping us in the light and out of Darkness. If we have taken the steps to secure eternity and have rendered ourselves Christians, through Jesus Christ, why would you wait another second to appropriate the Grace that is begging us to keep on the track to Eternity?

Hebrews 10:22-39 (AMP) The Original Writer:

Paul_X_Barnabas_Origen_**_ "let us approach [God] with a true and sincere heart in unqualified assurance of faith, having had our hearts sprinkled clean from an evil conscience and our bodies washed with pure water. **v23** Let us seize and hold tightly the confession of our hope without wavering, for He who promised is reliable and trustworthy and faithful [to His word]; **v24** and let us consider [thoughtfully] how we may encourage one another to love and do good deeds, **v25** not forsaking our meeting together [as believers for worship and instruction], as is the habit of some, but encouraging one another; and all the more [faithfully] as you see the day [Christ's return] approaching.

Christ or Judgment?

v26 For if we go on willfully and deliberately sinning after receiving the knowledge of the truth, there no longer remains a sacrifice [to atone] for our sins [that is, no further offering to anticipate], **v27** but a kind of awful and terrifying expectation of [divine] judgment and The Fury Of A Fire Burning Wrath which will Consume The Adversaries [those who pit themselves in opposition to God]. **v28** Anyone who has ignored and set aside the Law of Moses is put to death without mercy on the testimony of two or three witnesses. **v29** How much greater punishment do you think he will deserve who has rejected and trampled underfoot the Son of God, and has considered unclean and common the blood of the covenant that sanctified him, and has insulted the Spirit of Grace [who imparts the unmerited favor and blessing of God]? **v30** For we know Him who said, "Vengeance is Mine [retribution and the deliverance of justice rest with Me], I Will Repay [the wrongdoer]." And again, "The Lord Will Judge His People." **v31** It is a fearful and terrifying thing to fall into the hands of the Living God [incurring His Judgment and wrath]. **v32** But remember the earlier days, when, after being [spiritually] enlightened, you [patiently] endured a great conflict of sufferings, **v33** sometimes by being made a spectacle, publicly exposed to insults and distress, and sometimes by becoming companions with those who were so treated. **v34** For you showed sympathy and deep concern for those who were imprisoned, and you joyfully accepted the [unjust] seizure of your belongings and the confiscation of your property, conscious of the fact that you have a better possession, and a lasting one [prepared for you in heaven]. **v35** Do not, therefore, fling away [fearless] confidence, for it has a glorious and great reward. **v36** For you have need for patient endurance [to bear up under difficult circumstances without compromising], so that when you have carried out the will of God, you may receive and enjoy to the full what is promised. **v37** For yet in a very little while, He Who Is Coming Will Come. And Will Not Delay.

v38 But My Righteous One [the one justified by faith] Shall Live By Faith [respecting man's relationship to God and trusting Him]; And If He Draws Back [shrinking in fear], My Soul Has No Delight In Him. **v39** But our way is not of those who shrink back to destruction, but [we are] of those who believe [relying on God through Faith in Jesus Christ, the Messiah] and by this confident faith preserve the soul."

1.   I believe the Bible to be absolutely true to remarks made in it with few exceptions, to name one, would be the **church**. That means that what we read is what we should do. This book indicates what I saw wrong with the use of the word **church**. When it was originally set forth for William Tyndale to develop an original copy of the First Old English translation of the New Testament, it was completed by Tyndale in **A.D. 1525-26.** This copy was straight forward, honest and truthfully translated by Tyndale after he received an original copy as Jesus had requested, through His beloved spokesman, Matthew, one of the original Apostles who carried the finished book to Tyndale, I do not know for sure, so I will not comment on this!

The Instructions For Life Are Biblical Commandments!

2.   The Law was given through Moses. Grace and Faith came through God, Christ, and the Holy Spirit. These are instructions and directions to provide mankind a pattern of rights and wrongs, and many other lessons are included. What happens if a person through lack of Faith goes to the bottom of the barrel? He or she needs Grace, yet the person has failed to discover anything about Grace. He/she knows nothing about Grace. What happens next? You be the Author.

3.   Tell me what you are reading as I am writing in the following sentence: **Grace is the unmerited favor of God toward mankind!** Are you saying that no one but Christ or God with the help and assurance of the Holy Spirit can become a beacon of light and

salvation, instantaneously, for lost mankind? Yes! How right you are! Recall earlier in this Chapter this quotation: In Eph. 2:8-9, Paul states the free character of Grace perhaps even more explicitly, now not using the language of justification, but simply of salvation. **We are told that we have been saved "by Grace," but "through faith." Grace is seen here as the means by which we are saved, a free gift. Faith is seen as the mechanism by which that salvation or grace is appropriated.**

4.   Yes. You might be able, Almighty God and King Jesus permitting, to get down on your hands and knees and pray! I thought about it! The best answer, I believe, is to get down on your hands and knees and pray! Is this the 100th time that you have done this? Or is it the first? Do you think that God and Christ might just lean down, pick you up, and take you home? You know the chances of that! And My advice to You and to me, is we better start praying for forgiveness and mean it, all the way to the core! Which do you perceive to be the strongest mechanism of obedience and Christian love to God, Christ, and the Holy Spirit? Is it Faith or Grace or both?

        Which comes first, Faith or Grace and Why? If you have no faith in God, why would you worry about securing God's Grace? If you have Strong and Living Faith in Christ, why would you wait even one minute to ask for Grace from our Father in Heaven. I see the God-Head keeping us in the light and out of Darkness. If we have taken the steps to secure eternity and have rendered ourselves Christians through Jesus Christ, in Baptism and Obedience, Why would you wait another second to appropriate the Grace that is begging us to keep on the track to Eternity? Wait! I have an Idea:

5.   To **be able to appropriate Grace and Live A Life of Righteousness, we must deliberately focus on what the Bible really says about Faith, and then live our Faith. How strong is your Faith? How strong is your ability, with God's help and direction, in achieving Faith? Would you like to hear what I think I have found out for myself?** I am beginning to think that I sense a Tug of War between Faith and Grace! **If faith exceeds Grace where is the victory? If Grace exceeds Faith where is the victory?**

1) Red Team *If faith exceeds Grace where is the victory? If one's Faith grows stronger and stronger, why would we need more Grace? I am beginning to see the Light!

2) Blue Team *If Grace greatly exceeds Faith where is the victory? If one's Grace grows stronger and stronger, why would we need more Faith? I believe I am

beginning to see the Light!

If Faith (Red Team) greatly exceeds Grace (Blue Team), One's Faith may grow stronger and stronger! Faith is outgrowing Grace! In the Eyes of God, True or False? Likewise, if Grace (Blue Team) greatly exceeds Faith (Red Team), One's Grace grows stronger and Stronger! Grace is outgrowing Faith! In the eyes of God, True or False?

Two things are very much certain. We know that Red Faith Team generates Grace for the sake of appropriation and likewise Grace. Blue Team generates a more Faithlike person who is greatly desiring the eternal home with God, Christ and the Holy Spirit and anyone else that God invites into His eternity! Now that we have been searching the benefactors of Red and Blue teams, let us instead take hold of something that God and Christ left with us. **Do right and God will always stand with His team of Saints to Do the same.** If you are simply saying we need to do something for our salvation, be ready to say what you are doing? If you know not what to do, then don't do it! Keep in touch with the word **Appropriation**! Scripture follows that I especially like to use to remind all of us who are in need, and that dramatically means, all of us! Yes, we all want very much to become Partakers of the Divine Nature in **2nd Peter 1:3-11** (From the AMP Bible). "For His divine power has bestowed on us [absolutely] everything necessary for [a dynamic spiritual] life and godliness, through true and personal knowledge of Him who called us by His own glory and excellence. **v4** For by these He has bestowed on us His precious and magnificent promises [of inexpressible value], so by then you may escape from the immoral freedom that is in the world because of disreputable desire and become sharers of the divine nature. **v5** For this very reason, applying your diligence [to the divine promises, make every effort] in exercising] your faith to, develop moral excellence, and in moral excellence, knowledge (insight, understanding), **v6** and in your knowledge, self-control, and in your self control, steadfastness, and in your steadfastness, godliness, **v7** and in your godliness, brotherly affection, and in your brotherly affection, [develop Christian] love [that is, learn to unselfishly seek the best for others and do things for their benefit]. **v8** For as these qualities are yours and are increasing [in you as you grow toward spiritual maturity], they will keep you from being useless and unproductive, in regard to the true knowledge and greater understanding of our Lord Jesus Christ. **v9** For whoever lacks these qualities is blind--short sighted [closing his spiritual eyes to the truth], having become oblivious to the fact that he was cleansed from his old sins. **v10** Therefore, believers, be all the more diligent to make certain about His calling and choosing you [be sure that your behavior reflects and confirms your relationship with God]; for by doing these things [actively developing these virtues], you will never stumble [in your spiritual growth and will live a life that leads others away from sin]; **v11** for in this way entry into the eternal Kingdom of our Lord and Savior Jesus Christ will be abundantly provided you."

Yet, if we sit back and refuse to do our part to keep our lives connected to Grace, we will witness our own downfall and never experience the real effects of Grace that God, Christ, and the Holy Spirit freely provided to us for a life of eternal Holiness.

Not only must we keep our eyes on Grace and be ready to request of God the Grace we need to develop fully for eternal life, we must continually keep our minds active in our efforts to keep all of the commandments of the God-Head. Grace and Biblical commandments are to work together. We look for the commandments that are dutifully yours and mine, recorded in the Words of God and His Son, as both are assisted by the Holy Spirit. The fulfillment of these commands feeds us the ingredients of an active life in Eternity prepared by God, Christ and the Holy Spirit and all mankind charged with productive efforts to listen to the Father, the Son and the Holy Spirit for Direction and Continual Solace in the Hereafter.

We have only touched the baseline in **Faith, Holiness and Love!** May I encourage you to use much of your time in Bible Study and learn to sense the very strong and meaningful words of God, Jesus, and the Holy Spirit! God has promised us Life, Ever After, if we follow the Commandments of those listed above. Each one of the Three above has a Mighty Work to finish, and you and I, still alive today have an extremely important part to play in our own Salvation that takes us to the Promised Land.

In **1ˢᵗ Corinthians 12:13-14,** we read, "For by [means of the personal agency of] one [Holy] Spirit we were all, whether Jews or Greeks, slaves or free, baptized [and by baptism united together] into one body, and all made to drink of one Holy Spirit. **v14** For the body does not consist of one limb or organ but of many."

1ˢᵗ Corinthians 15:25-28 "For [Christ] must be King and reign until He has put all [His] enemies under His feet.[4] **v26** The last enemy to be subdued and abolished is death. **v27** For He [the Father] has put all things in subjection to His [Christ's] feet. But when it says, All things are put in subjection [under Him], it is evident that He [Himself] is excepted Who does the subjecting of all things to Him.[5] **v28** However, when everything is subjected to Him, then the Son Himself will also subject Himself to [the Father] Who put

---

[4] Psalm 110:1 The Lord (Father) says to my Lord (the Messiah, His Son),"Sit at My right hand Until I make Your enemies a footstool for Your feet [subjugating them into complete submission]."
[5] Psalm 8:6 You made him to have dominion over the works of Your hands; You have put all things under his feet,

all things under Him, so that God may be all in all [be everything to everyone, supreme, the indwelling and controlling factor of life]."

Chapter Six

Sermon On The Real Meaning Of (Faith - Holiness – Love)

In Matthew 3:13-17 "Then Jesus came from Galilee to the Jordan to John to be baptized by Him. v14 But John "protested strenuously, having in mind to prevent Him saying, It is I who have need to be baptized by You, and so You come to Me?" v15 But Jesus replied to Him, Permit it just now, for this is the fitting way for [both of] us to fulfill all righteousness [that is, to perform completely whatever is right]. Then, He permitted Him. v16 And when Jesus was baptized, He went up at once out of the water, and behold the Heavens were opened, and he [John] saw the Spirit of God descending like a dove and lighting on Him. v17 And behold, a voice from heaven said, This is my Son, My Beloved, in Whom I delight!"[6] [7]

Yet, another perspective: Matt. 22:37-39 "And He Replied to him, You shall love the Lord your God with all Your Heart and with all your soul and with all your mind." Now let's look at a follow-up of verse 38 and 39 of this very solid subject. v38 "This is the great (most important, principal) and first commandant. v39 And a second is like it: You shall love your neighbor as [you do] yourself."[8] This episode continues through verse 46. Let's read the continuation from verse 40 that follows:

Matt. 22:40-46 "These two commandments sum up and upon them depend all the Law and the Prophets. v41 Now while the pharisees were still assembled there, Jesus asked them a question, v42 Saying, "What do you think of the Christ? Whose Son is He?" They said to Him, The Son of David. v43 He said to them, "How is it then that David, under the influence of the [Holy] Spirit, calls Him Lord, saying, v44, The Lord said to my Lord, Sit at My right hand until I put Your enemies under Your feet?" v45 If then David thus calls Him the Lord, how is He his Son? v46 And no one was able to answer Him a word, nor from that day did anyone venture or dare to question Him."

---

[6] Psalm 2:7 "I will declare the decree of the Lord: He said to Me, 'You are My Son; This day [I proclaim] I have begotten You.

[7] Isaiah 42:1 "Behold, My Servant, whom I uphold; My Chosen One *in whom* My soul delights. I have put My Spirit upon Him; He will bring forth justice to the nations.

[8] Leviticus 19:18 You shall not take revenge nor bear any grudge against the sons of your people, but you shall love your neighbor (acquaintance, associate, companion) as yourself; I am the Lord.

Matt. 17:1-5 "And six days later after this, Jesus took with Him Peter and James and John the brother of James and led them up on a high mountain by themselves. **v2** And His appearance underwent a change in their presence; and His face shone clear and bright like the sun, and His clothing became as white as light. **v3** And behold, there appeared to them Moses and Elijah, who kept talking with Him. **v4** Then Peter began to speak and said to Jesus, Lord, it is good and delightful that we are here; If You approve, I will put up three booths here--one for You and one for Moses and one for Elijah. **v5** While he was still speaking behold a shining cloud [composed of light] overshadowed them, and a voice from the cloud said, **This is My Son, My beloved, with whom I am [and have always been] delighted! Listen to Him!**" Are we listening? Is the world Listening? If not, Why not? God has just communicated an important message to the World, and you and I have heard it, and we understand it! What did He just say to His Son Jesus Christ, and this has echoed around the world time and time again. You know what He said, and I know what He said and the whole world should know what He said. Yet, billions of human beings have heard and have refused to listen to His words! When our Lord says something, we strain our ears to hear, but are we really listening?

In verses 36-40 of the **Book of Matthew, Chapter 22,** great efforts were expended to get some response from various sects of humans. You wanted a bit of information, but as you listen as you read, you will say to yourself that no one is really listening! Are your ears and my ears really tuned in to God and/or Jesus Himself? **Matt. 22:37** was communicated from the mouth of our Savior! Did his audience hear what was said? Listen carefully!

v36 "Teacher, which kind of commandment is great and important (the principal kind) in the Law? [Some commandments are light--which are heavy?] v37 And He replied to him, you shall love the Lord your God with all your heart and with all of your soul and with all of your mind (intellect). v38 This is the great (most important, principal) and first commandment. v39 And a second is like it: You shall love your neighbor as [you do yourself.] v40 These two commandments sum up and depend upon all the Law and the Prophets."

Wow, that is powerful! "Love God and your Neighbor as yourself." One minute, Lord! I don't even know my neighbors. **Whose fault is that?** But Lord, we have nothing in common? **How do you know?** But Lord? **THE LORD SAID, "LOVE YOUR NEIGHBOR AS YOURSELF"!** How do we show love to those whom we do not know? Perhaps we let our attitude show! We do little things. Such as...? Well, we can collect and stack their newspaper when they are out of town. We could call them when we go to the store and ask them if we can bring something to them. These are small things aren't they? Yes, things done with the right attitude may add up to God's way of looking at things we could do for our neighbors. **Little things done with the right attitude of "Love Thy Neighbor," may mean a lot to our God. Perhaps, Much Much More Than We Might Think!**

1st John, Chapter 4:7-16 and Chapter 5:1-21 could provide for an outstanding attitude change on the part of all of us. **1st John 4:7-16** "Beloved, let us love one another, for love is (springs) from God; and he who loves [his fellowman] is begotten (born) of God and is coming [progressively] to know and understand God [to perceive and recognize and get a better and clearer knowledge of Him]. **v8** He who does not love has not become acquainted with God [does not and never did know Him], for God is love. **v9** In this the Love of God was made manifest (displayed) where we are concerned: in that God sent His Son, the only begotten or unique [Son], into the world that we might live through Him. **v10** In this is love: not that we loved God, but that He loved us and sent His Son to be the propitiation (the atoning sacrifice) for our sins. **v11** Beloved, if God loved us so [very much], we also ought to love one another. **v12** No man has at any time [yet] seen God. But if we love one another, God abides (lives and remains) in us and His love (that love which is essentially His) is brought to completion (to its full maturity, runs its full course, is perfected) in us! **v13** By this we come to know (perceive, recognize, and understand) that we abide (live and remain) in Him and He in us: because He has given (imparted) to us of His [Holy] Spirit. **v14** And [besides] we ourselves have seen (have deliberately and steadfastly contemplated) and bear witness that the Father has sent the Son [as the] Savior of the World. **v15** Anyone who confesses (acknowledges, owns) that Jesus is the Son of God, abides (lives, makes His home) in him and he [abides, lives, makes his home] in God. **v16** And we know (understand, recognize, are conscious of, by observation and by experience) and believe (adhere to, and put faith in and rely on) the love God cherishes for us. God is love, and he who dwells and continues in love dwells and continues in God, and God dwells and continues in him."

In 1st John, Chapter 5, verses 1-21 "Everyone Who believes (adheres to, trusts, and relies on the fact) that Jesus is the Christ (the Messiah) is a born-again child of God; and everyone who loves the Father also loves the one born of Him (His offspring). **v2** By this we come to know (recognize and understand) that we love the children of God: when we love God and obey His commands (orders-charges)--[when we keep His ordinances and are mindful of His precepts and His teaching]. **v3** For the [true] love of God is this: that we do His commands [keep His ordinances and are mindful of His precepts and teaching]. And these orders of His are not irksome (burdensome, oppressive, or grievous). **v4** For whatever is born of God is victorious over the world; and this is the victory that conquers the world, even our faith. **v5** Who is it that is victorious over [that conquers] the world but he who believes that Jesus is the Son of God [who adheres to, trusts in, and relies on that fact]? **v6** This is He Who came by (with) water and blood [His baptism and His death], Jesus Christ (the Messiah)-- not by (in) the water only, but by (in) the water and the blood. And it is the [Holy] Spirit Who bears witness, because the [Holy] Spirit is the Truth. **v7** So there are three witnesses in Heaven: the Father, the Word, and the Holy Spirit, and these three are One; **v8** and there are three witnesses on earth: the Spirit, the water, and the blood: and these three agree [are in unison; their testimony coincides]. **v9** If we accept [as we do] the testimony of men [if we are willing to take human authority], the testimony of God is greater (of stronger authority), for this is the testimony of God, even the witness which He has borne regarding His Son. **v10** He who believes in the Son of God [who adheres to, trusts in, and relies on Him] has the testimony [possesses this divine attestation] within himself. He who does not believe God [in this way] has made Him out to be and represented Him as a liar, because he has not believed (put his faith in, adhered to, and relied on) the evidence (the testimony) that God has borne regarding His Son. **v11** And this is that testimony (that evidence): God gave us eternal life, and this life is in His Son. **v12** He who possesses the Son has that life; he who does not possess the Son of God does not have that life. **v13** I write this to you who believe in (adhere to, trust in, and rely on) the name of the Son of God [in the peculiar services and blessings conferred by Him on men, so that you may know [with settled and absolute knowledge] that you [already] have life, yes, eternal life. **v14** And this is the confidence (the assurance, the privilege of boldness) which we have in Him: [we are sure] that if we ask anything (make any request) according to His will (in agreement with His own plan), He listens to, and hears us. **v15** And if (since) we [positively] know that He listens to us in whatever we ask, we also know [with settled and absolute knowledge] that we have [granted us as our present possessions] the requests made of Him. **v16** If anyone sees His brother [believer] committing a sin that does not [lead to] death (the extinguishing of life), he will pray and [God] will give him Life [yes, He will grant life to all those whose sin is not one leading to death].There is a sin [that leads] to death; I do not say that one should pray for that. **v17** All wrongdoing is sin, and there is sin which does not [involve] death [that may be repented of and forgiven] **v18** We know [absolutely] that anyone born of God does not [deliberately and knowingly] practice committing sin, but the One Who was begotten of God carefully watches over and protects him [Christ's divine presence within him preserves him against the evil], and the wicked one does not lay hold (get a grip) on him or touch [him]. **v19** We know [positively] that we are of God, and the whole world [around us] is under the power of the evil one.

v20 And we [have seen and] know [positively] that the Son of God has [actually] come to this world and has given us understanding and insight [progressively] to perceive (recognize) and come to know better and more clearly Him Who is true; and we are in Him Who is true--in His Son Jesus Christ (the Messiah). This Man is the true God and Life eternal. **v21** Little children, keep yourselves from idols (false gods) [from anything and everything that would occupy the place in your heart due to God, from any sort of substitute for Him that would take first place in your life]." Amen (so let it be).

What a Great chapter! Yet, we must read this material again and again! For now, we must close, but for your sake and my sake we shall read these words again and again, in our time, to continue life on earth! However, I would like to close it with a favorite in the **15th Chapter** of the **Book of John, verses 9-17.** Jesus is speaking: "I have loved you [just] as the Father has loved Me: abide in my love [continue in His love with Me]. **v10** If you keep My commandments [if you continue to obey my instructions], you will abide in My love and live on in it, just as I have obeyed My Father's Commandments and live on in His love. **v11** I have told you these things that My joy and delight may be in you, and that your joy and gladness may be of full measure and complete and overflowing. **v12** This is my Commandment: that you love one another [just] as I have loved you. **v13** No one has greater love [no one has shown stronger affection] than to lay down (give up) his own life for his friends. **v14** You are My friends if you keep on doing the things which I command you to do. **v15** I do not call you servants (slaves) any longer, for the servant does not know what his Master is doing (working out). But I have called you My friends, because I have made known to you everything that I have heard from my Father. [I have revealed to you everything that I have learned from Him.] **v16** You have not chosen Me, but I have chosen you and I have appointed you [I have planted you], that you might go and bear fruit and keep on bearing, that your fruit may be lasting [that it may remain, abide], so that whatever you ask the Father in My name [as presenting all that I AM], He may give it to you. **v17** This is what I command you: that you love one another."

Chapter Seven

What Has This Book Done For Me? What Will It Do For You?

I didn't completely plan it this way, but it came together in such a way that I am supremely pleased with the results. It all started about five years ago. That is when I published my First Edition. My publisher (Xulon Press) did everything just right. When I saw that they gave me sound advice (just as they had told me), there was not much to do except take it and thank them! If they suggested to do it their way, I assure you that it would always look much better than my way.

If you have read this book to this point, be assured that it will become a book that has brought new changes, even from the last edition. It's a book that has slightly changed my mind about several things. However, I find these changes have spoken exactly as I should have many years ago. And now my story of change has come of age.

Please understand that nothing has changed for the reason that anyone ever told me that certain changes were needed. That may sound crazy, but believe me, it was my own duty to make the change due to a King in A.D. 1611. The materials set forth in this book, Chapters One through Ten, have brought genuine purpose to this writing that proves beyond the shadow of a doubt that Jesus died so mankind could live. May I elaborate?

I Will Build My Ekklesia! Jesus did not want a (**church** or a Church building) as very few of us who worship Him have learned. The story of what Jesus really said in Matt. 16:18 is, "...**I will build My (What ?)**" From about age 12 through age 84, I have labored for the Lord with what I hope were good intentions and worthy efforts of love! However, I was very fortunate to begin to count my blessings once I was able and amazed **by what I saw in Matt. 16:18 "...I will build My Ekklesia..."**

Jesus has spoken! The Ekklesia is the English equivalent of the Greek word ἐκκλησία. **This word translates to Congregation and\or Assembly. It should never apply to the word church!** Before we leave this section, we need to spend a very short time and lend another glance to reinforce our minds with actions taken by, what I would call a Bully King, King James 1ˢᵗ!

Again, please keep in mind the word ἐκκλησία never converts to the English word **church**. What King James 1ˢᵗ and his cohorts did was to dig way back to around 675 B.C. and found the word for **church** used at that time. There are some Bibles described in this book that did stick with the word that Jesus used, that being ekklesia, or better yet, in **Koine Greek, ἐκκλησία, meaning (Congregation) and\or (Assembly).** To have made it look accurate, King James and his boys decided to use the word **church** of about 675 B.C. This Greek word is **Kuriakon, and was the root of the word church, in language altogether different than what Jesus spoke while on earth, 1st Century A.D.** They could have used this many years ago and very few people would have ever known. **And do you know what? They could and did! It, in most cases is well hidden. But we must assume that most Bible publishers know this, and perhaps forget about it, as Bibles continue to roll off the shelves. My First Edition listed three different Bibles on pages 34 & 35 that were published correctly, setting an example for how others should publish today, but don't. They are the Tyndale Bible, Young's Literal Translation and the World English Bible.**

You see, I was a proud member of the Body of Christ and very proud to be identified as part of the Church of Christ. I studied long and hard and tried to find the full truth and nothing but the truth. Then I remembered reading about 56-58 years ago, a book written by Dr. Riddley Stroop. This tells me a new story!

I didn't like what I was hearing. It just didn't sound correct. About 5 years ago, I wrote what I guess could be classified as the First Edition of this book and published it, but I had very little time to go further into the life and the wonderful writings of William Tyndale. It bothered me that I had not completely finished the book, so three years ago I decided to complete it! I am now consumed with this Edition of the Book that says unto us, **"thou arte Peter: and upon this Rocke I wyll byll my congregacion..."** What a shock it was to me! I had no idea. **A friend asked, what do we need to do? I sat amazed and said You have been baptized, have you not? Yes! You have listened to God, Christ and the Holy Spirit. You have studied the Bible and you are a Christian. All we need to do in my humble opinion after getting this far is to Continue to live our devoted lives to the God-Head! We understand the workings of the Holy Spirit and admit that we have much more to absorb. We are requesting a bit more study time!**

In 1ˢᵗ Cor. 16:19 we read, "The congregacions of Asia salute you. Aquila and Priscilla salute you mouch in the Lorde and so doeth the congregacion that is in their housse." William Tyndale penned this for the first Bible (A.D. 1525-26) in English that was stand-alone.

Does this **congregacion** sound like a well-built castle with some kind of house attached to it? **No!** I would say they are each living in their home or house and they have all of their services, etc. within the confines of their home. Additionally, they will have every visitor to stay with them for time needed together. It would be like living in the country, walking a few miles to a building owned by the community and going to two services on Sundays whenever speakers are available to walk to the services out from a given location or elsewhere to preach the Gospel of Christ. Yes, sermons have been preached in houses!

Let's journey now to a **Congregation** or an **Assembly** of Christians, so that we might solidify a choice-decision of the God-Head regarding the Body of Christ. We now realize that we need to look at the Body of Christ as opposed to the Church of Christ. Some important information is obtained from the early writings of William Tyndale in his material that he was developing into the first "stand-alone" version in the English Language. We need to become concerned about Christ and His relationship with the **Body of Christ, His followers, including you and me! Col. 1:18 says, "And he is the heed of the body that is to wit of the congregacion: he is the begynnynge an fyrst begotten of the deed that in all thynges He might have the preeminence." The Amplified version did a very good job of developing this into English that we can all read and enjoy, except for the word church. That is not a correct rendition of the English word for: Koine Greek, Acts 20:28, and/or Eph. 5:25-27 meaning (Congregation) and\or (Assembly).** However, permit me to develop this scripture to be available in print for many years, in the Amplified Bible, to make my point. **Col. 1:18 Amplified Version: "He also is the Head of [His] body, the church, (should have been Congregacion or Assembly for correctness) seeing that He is the Beginning, the Firstborn among the dead, so that He alone in everything and in every respect might occupy the chief place [stand first and be preeminent]."**

The bottom line is Love one another! Love the Father, Love the Messiah (Jesus), and Love the Holy Spirit. Now this is great, and Jesus told us to love one another. And besides the Three there are plenty to love. Fellow Christians! Who are they? They are current members of the Body of Christ mixed in with other such Body of Christ members with differing names. Yet, above all, I have quickly changed to try my very best to love all others who show up, but may not show us their love. Must they show us their love first? Absolutely not! We must carry the word of God with us. We must love them first, and forever! We must live with Christ!

Above all: Include as many people that God, Christ and the Holy Spirit direct us to include, to help and to give the right answers for those who may harbor the wrong answers. Let us forever keep prayer available for those who may call themselves Christians. Tell me where we might find Christians? In **Congregations** in every part of our World. This would include many, to name a very very few below!

Congregations of Christ - Congregations of Baptists – Congregations of Methodists - Congregations of Lutherans - Congregations of Presbyterians and many other Congregations

To sit and view the congregations of Christians on this page looks to me a bit strange. Mankind does not make the selection of members of the Body of Christ except by the way they live for God, Christ, and the Holy Spirit! The God-Head will select Christians, regardless of what we call ourselves. They are the only ones who are able to say, "Welcome, good and faithful servants!" You See! They can read our hearts!

They may say, "We recognize every soul before us based upon their positive life, undertakings for readiness for Heaven and their love for Us and Mankind! Enter into Eternal Life!" Are we living with New Perspectives: Changing slightly from what we have been doing to what we believe is a bit more scriptural. We believe that this too, is what Jesus Christ intended! If this were not true, I assure you I would not be proofreading this document! Believe me, my Faith tells me over and over that this is the correct way!

Jesus is the King, The Messiah of the Body of Christians. Every Christian that is saved by Christ and/or Almighty God will be in Heaven. There has been a huge mistake on the part of King James getting the word **church** in place of **Assembly** and/or **Congregacion**, but those of Faith, Holiness and Love are a big part of the Body of Christ, just as you and I are. No one except our God and our Savior, Jesus Christ, will be permitted to make changes, lest it be the Holy Spirit with concurrence by God and our Messiah. Therefore, I enclose the following paragraph. Permit me to tell something of the story! **I would admit that there is undoubtedly a small body of Christians with homes at this time, who are convinced that God, Christ, and the Holy Spirit have changed our feelings about this new surge: We believe for the betterment of our Eternal lives!**

That the (one Congregation and/or Assembly of Christ) is only a small part of a larger mass of Congregations and/or Assemblies throughout the world, (several were named earlier) who are attempting to care for Christians and help guide them in their midst, to eternity. Wouldn't it be wonderful to view and hear a worldwide convention whereby all **Congregations** and or **Assemblies** of Christ (or whatever they

64

would be named), as they help ready all members of the Body of Christ that may be worshiping together for a great Eternity!

The following is a biblical call-out of scripture that gives attention to the Gospel of Christ, Commandments of God and Christ and the Holy Spirit, and God's Words about the Obedience to those Commandments! I came across a word that really made me a very happy Christian.

Find now please, the translations by William Tyndale in 1st Cor. 7:17, which stated, "...but even as God hath distributed to every man. As the Lord has called every person so let him walke: and so ordern I in all congregacions." And then I got an answer for something that I had been wanting to rediscover and learn much more about. For some reason I continued to read two more verses, which brought me face to face with the words **"Commandments of God" in 1st Cor. 7:19**.

It was a happy and great day for yours truly. Here is why! I had begun to hear local Christians in various places talk considerably about the way that many souls in Congregations of Christ around the USA felt places of worship were somewhat in lockout.

I agree that the Death, Burial, and Resurrection of Christ was one of the most significant events ever, as well as encompassing the life of our God, our Savior, Jesus Christ, and the Holy Spirit. I also believe this event is rightfully called the Gospel of Jesus Christ, our Savior! And were we not presented a question about Christian baptism? Yes, no doubt about it! I do have a question of all the Saints within reading distance of the Gospel of Christ as set forth below. **For Christians or those who are thinking about becoming a Christian in the future: Which do you believe to be the most important scripture below (#1 #2 or #3) for Christians?**

Scripture #1: Hebrews 5:9 "And [His completed experience] making Him perfectly [equipped], He became the Author and Source of eternal salvation to all those who give heed and obey Him."

Scripture #2: 1st Cor. 7:17 "Only, let each one [seek to conduct himself and regulate his affairs so as to lead the life which the Lord has allotted and imparted to him and to which God has invited and summoned him.] This should be the order of the day in all congregations of Christ."

Scripture #3: 1st Cor. 7:19 "For circumcision is nothing and counts for nothing, neither does uncircumcised, but [what counts is] keeping the Commandments of God."

A word about these scriptures above: Hearing the indication in the Bible about directions from our God and our Christ and the Holy Spirit on the Commandments, Blessed Instructions of Life, given to us, indicate to me that they are to be applied till we die and are taken to Eternity at the appropriate time. And to do so leaves a good taste in the mouths of Christians. Not to do so would seem to me to violate the word of God, Jesus the Savior, and the Holy Spirit! These words are in extremely important stated sentences, by and for so many Christians! Is it because all people that name Christ as their Savior and know why, wish to express this fact to them in a world-catching way, one way or another? Is this the correct thing to do? As you have picked up within my written words from God's Words, Christ Jesus our Savior, as a result of the Guidance and Actions Performed by God Almighty, is by God's choice, the Author of many parts of the Holy Bible. Occasionally, God Himself will engage in His Holy Words of Bliss and Wisdom, as indicated by the hands and thoughts of the translators.

May I summarize what I believe about the structure of congregations and their places of worship. I have chosen descriptions of the words written in the Amplified Topical Reference Bible.[9] This material originates from pg. 222 of the Concordance under section (D), entitled Characteristics of The New Testament Church (should be Congregacions per Tyndale and/or Assemblies). The following scriptures in normal print have been cited and can be looked up at your leisure, but scriptures in bold represent the full text.

Characteristics Of New Testament Congregations Around The World Showing Precisely Jesus Christ As Our Savior

1.   Saved by Christ's Blood

Eph. 5:25-27 and **Acts 20:28 "Take care and be on guard for yourselves and the whole flock over which the Holy Spirit has appointed you bishops and guardian to shepherd (tend and feed and guide) the (church) of the Lord or of God which He obtained for Himself [buying it and saving it for Himself] with His own blood."** In Acts 20:28, the word **church** should have appeared as it originally was, either **Congregation** and or **Assembly**, 86 years prior to it being changed to **church**. Do you think that Jesus would suddenly, 86 years after it had been announced,

---

[9] Copyright 1954, 1958, 1962, 1964, 1965, 1987 by the Lockman Foundation, All rights reserved. Used by permission. Amplified Topical Index, Copyright 2006, Published by Zondervan - Grand Rapids, Michigan 49530, USA - Library of Congress Catalog Card Number 2005934717

print or change it? I do not believe Jesus had this changed! I hope readers agree!

2. Usually Met in Homes

Col. 4:15 and **Romans 16:5 "[Remember me] also to the church [that meets]in their house. Greet my beloved Epaenetus, who was a first fruit (first convert) to Christ in Asia."** The word **church** should be removed! Not in the original.

3. Held Worship Services

Acts 20:7, 1ˢᵗ Cor. 14:26-28 and **Heb. 10:25 "Not forsaking or neglecting to assemble together [as believers], as is the habit of some people, but admonishing (warning, urging, and encouraging) one another, and all the more faithfully as you see the day approaching."**

4. Baptism and Lord's Supper

Baptism: 1ˢᵗ Cor. 12:13 and **Acts 18:8 "But Crispus, the leader of the synagogue, believed [that Jesus is the Messiah and acknowledged Him with Joyful trust as Savior and Lord], together with his entire household; and many of the Corinthians who listened [to Paul also] believed and were baptized."**

Lord's Supper: Acts 2:42 and **1ˢᵗ Cor. 11:24-25 "And when He had given Thanks, He broke [it] and said, *Take, Eat.* This is My body, which is broken for you. Do this to call Me [affectionately] to remembrance. v25 Similarly when supper was ended, He took the cup also, saying, This cup is the new covenant [ratified and established] in My blood. Do this, as often as you drink [it], to call Me [affectionately to remembrance.]"**

5. Experienced Unity

One Body: Eph. 4:13 and **Rom. 12:5 "So we, numerous as we are, are one body in Christ (the Messiah) and individually we are parts one of another [mutually dependent on one another]."**

One Flock/One Shepherd: John 10:16 "And I have other sheep [beside these] that are not of this fold. I must bring and impel those also; and they will listen to My voice and heed My call, and so there will be [they will become] one flock under one Shepherd."

6. Enjoyed Fellowship

1st John 1:3-7 and **Acts 2:42 "And they steadfastly persevered, devoting themselves constantly to the instruction and fellowship of the apostles, to the breaking of bread [including the Lord's Supper] and prayers."**

7. Helped Each Other

2nd Cor. 8:1-5 and **Acts 4:32-37 "Now the company of believers was of one heart and soul, and not one of them claimed that anything which he possessed was [exclusively] his own, but everything they had was in common and for the use of all. v33 And with great strength and ability and power the apostles delivered their testimony to the resurrection of the Lord Jesus, and great grace (loving-kindness and favor and goodwill) rested richly upon them all. v34 Nor was there a destitute or needy person among them, for as many as were owners of lands or houses proceeded to sell them, and one by one they brought (gave back) the amount received from the sales v35 And laid it at the feet of the apostles (special messengers). Then distribution was made according as anyone had need. v36 Now Joseph, a Levite and a native of Cyprus who was surnamed Barnabas by the apostles, which interpreted means Son of Encouragement, v37 Sold a field which belonged to him and brought the sum of money and laid it at the feet of the apostles."**

8. Evangelized Others

Rom. 1:8 "First, I thank my God through Jesus Christ for all of you, because [the report of] your faith is made known to all the world and is commended everywhere."

9. Grew

Acts 4:4, Acts 5:4 and **Acts 16:5 "So the churches were strengthened and made firm in the faith, and they increased in number day after day."** Congregacions (per Tyndale) and Assemblies are composed of the people that live, breathe and grow in spirit and truth. They die and then they go to account for their good life and meet face to face with God, Christ and The Holy Spirit! The word **churches** should not be here.

10. Was Organized

Phil. 1:1, 1st Tim. 3:1-13, Tit. 1:5-9 and **Acts 14:23 "And when they had appointed and ordained elders for them in each church with prayer and fasting, they** committed them to the Lord in Whom they had come to believe [being full of joyful trust that He is the Christ, the Messiah]." The word **church** needs to be changed, either to **Congregation** and/or **Assembly**.

11.   Had Problem

1st Cor. 1:11-12 "For it has been made clear to me, my brethren, by those of Chloe's household, that there are contentions and wrangling and factions among you. v12 What I mean is this, that each one of you [either] says, I belong to Paul, or I belong to Apollos, or I belong to Cephas (Peter), or I belong to Christ."

12.   Had to Exercise Discipline

1st Cor. 5:1-5, 2nd Thess. 3:11-15 and **Tit. 3:10-11** "[As for] a man who is factious [a heretical sectarian and cause of divisions], after admonishing him a first and second time, reject [him from your fellowship and have nothing more to do with him], v11 Well aware that such a person has utterly changed (is perverted and corrupted); he goes on sinning [though he] is convicted of guilt and self-condemned."

13.   Experienced Persecution

1st Thess. 2:14 and **1st Thess. 2:15** "Who killed both the Lord Jesus and the prophets, and harassed and drove us out, and continue to make themselves hateful and offensive to God and to show themselves foes of all men,"

Chapter Eight

Shall We Merge Our Qualifications With The One Worldwide Body?

Think for a Moment. Is it our place to say, "Merge with all religious units in the World at this very Moment. Who rules us at this very moment? Let it be: God, Christ, The Holy Spirit, and only others who believe and obey our Lord And Savior, are in prayer without ceasing, with the Word of God guiding their every step."

At times we may tend to observe the Good and the Bad! At times I tend to think that some Christians Make God's Methods seem to sound much more to the point. Remember, the Untested Points do not always serve mankind well. If this were so, Why would God make an everlasting positive direction in His Abode, instead of creations of godliness death rows that may have been from the hands of the Devil himself. Only God, Jesus Our Savior, The Holy Spirit along with the Born-Again have the answers.

What Would You Do With These Words?

Most of us have very good **congregation**s in our area. Have You Ever made a statement such as the following, that may lead to other such words? "Do we need to bring back the style and truth of New Testament Christianity?" Why do you say yes or no?

1ˢᵗ Cor. 2:12-13 "Now we have not received the spirit [that belongs to] the world, but the [Holy] Spirit Who is from God, [given to us] that we might realize and comprehend and appreciate the gifts [of divine favor and blessing so freely and lavishly] bestowed on us by God. v13 And we are setting these truths forth in words not taught by human wisdom but taught by the [Holy] Spirit, combining and interpreting spiritual truths with spiritual language [to those who possess the Holy Spirit]."

This passage of Scripture is only a beginning for readers to master and begin to identify parts of the kind, cited as examples that may be followed to continue to seek the Eternal Life. We will return to similar comments later!

I recognize that the starting point is to help all current and non-Christians, focus upon the first chore. That is a very difficult job in my humble opinion! Those of us who are currently satisfied with what we have done for the Word through the years, to assist what now seems to be appropriate, have got to take one step that seems impossible. **That step being, to accept the fact that we held tightly to words in many Bibles that were not apparently as appropriate as we may have thought.**

For example, many Christians felt as though we should latch on to teachings within our **congregations** to embrace the word **church**. Many have now learned that most Bibles that were for sale, or at least those printed with correct words, do not exist in large quantities. Every Bible we had in the building had the word **church** in it. We cannot start out properly until we have correct Bibles, can we? No! Little did we realize that a King named King James 1ˢᵗ, in A.D. 1611, changed the word from how it was given to William Tyndale in A.D. 1525-26, which he then (Tyndale) secured a proper development of words to affect the words that Jesus used in His preaching while here on earth. The King told his field of translators that they were to use the wrong key words for the word **church**, instead of using what Tyndale used, words that were in his hands for proper distribution to the masses, so the word **church** would not be used in any new edition.

Our understanding agrees with many, if not all of the professionally trained translators at the time and even today, long after these times have faded into incorrect words, which in essence caused the word **church** to be a dominant, but incorrectly used word. It mattered not that the word **church** was incorrectly used and the words that Tyndale had used (ekklesia— ἐκκλησία.,—**Congregation—Assembly**) were stricken from what had been used for over 86 years, prior to the wrong usage of these words that stopped the mature thoughts of many. Here is what the result led to. Tyndale, in following words that I believe Jesus first used on earth, did his work from which sprang the correct translation of the Gospel of Jesus Christ. This brought about a new, very usable translation of words that lent themselves to two words that could be used. These two words mentioned above, which Jesus spoke on earth, were translated to **Congregation** and/or **Assembly**, either one, being correctly used, to tell the Story of our Savior. The word that King James 1ˢᵗ used incorrectly and on purpose, was **church**. Based upon all facts of truth, our signs of meeting places, i.e. Churches of Christ, should now read as either **Congregation of Christ** or **Assembly of Christ!**

Perhaps a new sign on the outside of the building should be a part of restructuring, displaying the words, **A Congregation of Christ Meets Here. It is so simple to say, yet at first, so difficult to say it after all the years of meeting as a member of the Church of Christ. But it quickly is usable and should be used frequently to worship the God-Head, if and when accomplished.** In theory and only at this time of change when the new Congregation of Christ is recognized, advertised, and localized, can we begin to make new

72

strides in God's World that I sincerely think should have been done from the beginning. Jesus did it by speaking live on the Promised Eternity! Our Lord, and (William Tyndale, being appointed by Jesus and/or His lineage of Apostles to translate His words), used strong efforts of Faith to bring the first real spiritual breath of language, sprinkled with the words of Christ for consumption for all the earth and its inhabitants! This was made possible as you well know, by the printing press! So many things have changed or are in the process of changing!

Today, Christians should address some of the real differences in what was occurring in the Book of Acts and other locations in New Testament times, prior to the beginning of King James 1st deliberately misusing words and scripture that Jesus had used correctly. In other words, we address Christians worshiping God as set forth in words in current Bibles that have been entirely corrected, so as to address the true words spoken by Christ on earth. **Christians Should Be In Action To Bring Back The Style And Truth of Scripture Developed by God, Christ, and The Holy Spirit!**

I believe you will find extremely good reading for what we are about to propose in **1st Corinthians**, Chapters 2, 3, 4, 5, and 6. These are chapters that many people avoid. After you read these five chapters, I would like to make a few relevant remarks about this material.

Let's begin to look at a few of the verses in this great book. It is a book that I believe every Christian around the world should read a minimum of two times per year, just to be reminded of what is really important in God's World.

Starting with the **12th verse of the Second Chapter of the Book of 1st Corinthians.** God is talking to you and me in a very auspicious way! This word in almost every dictionary means **promising success!**

1st Cor. 2:12-13 "Now we have not received the spirit [that belongs to] the world, but the [Holy] Spirit Who is from God, [given to us] that we might realize and comprehend and appreciate the gifts [of divine favor and blessing so freely and lavishly] bestowed on us by God. v13 And we are setting these truths forth in words not taught by human wisdom but taught by the [Holy] Spirit, combining and interpreting spiritual truths with spiritual language [to those who possess the Holy Spirit]." Verse 14 goes on to say that a nonspiritual man is incapable of interpreting what the Holy Spirit is saying to those of the Faith and Love that Jesus has taught us. It is received, but not meaningful to him or her. Verse 15 says that the spiritual person understands the meaning of words from the Holy Spirit. Then verse 16 says, **"For who has known or understood the mind (the counsels and purposes) of the Lord so as to guide and instruct Him and give Him knowledge. But we have the mind of Christ (the Messiah) and, do hold the thoughts (feelings and purposes) of His heart."**[10] Now read **Rom. 12:1-21 and Rom. 13, 14, 15 and 16.**

Think about a **congregation** having the basic language that Tyndale developed from words spoken by Jesus in His days on earth before He was crucified on the cross for you, me, and all who take advantage of His death that atoned for our sins. Eternal prayer for all people behooves us in our total search for the Love of God, Christ, and the Holy Spirit!

God has spoken to many of His Converts, Christians who have recently come to know **that we are hoping to become a part of changing or restructuring the church into (Congregations of Christ)** wherever we may find the right people and the correct outlook! The language that Jesus and/or His representative provided for William Tyndale to translate were such words as **(ekklesia- ἐκκλησία,- Congregation-Assembly).** This was in A.D. 1525-26, yet as I have mentioned, they were stricken from the text that had been used for over 86 years prior to the wrong usage of words. Remember, the date of language change to carry out what King James 1st got the translators to do was in A.D. 1611.

Here are some final thoughts about Spiritual things! Jesus without a doubt understands completely what He meant by His statements about a One Worldwide **Congregation** and/or **Assembly** of Christ. God, His Son, and the Holy Spirit want us to be the Children of God and enjoy life ever after!

In simple language, in simplistic style and in all of Heavens' glory, Jesus told us what He was going to build. He did NOT use the word for **church**. The word that was dear to His heart and soul and what He directed Tyndale to write was His **(Congregations and/or Assemblies of people) called Christians**, who chose to follow Him!

Yes, this could be the beginning of the Congregacion/ Congregation and/or Assembly of Christ, commonly known as the Church of Christ! Those who found God and His son, and who once described what He was going to build, were those who would spend Eternity with all the Saints, along with God, Christ our Savior and the

---

[10] See **Isa. 40:13** and **Rom. 11:34**

Holy Spirit. His death upon the cross was our way to be with Them forever and ever. He saw to it that those of us who follow Him would be baptized into Him for the remission of sin.

Hypothetically speaking, now it's time to find a leader for the Congregation of Christ and we need to look no further. Someone said, "Yes"? "Yes" with a question mark? **Yes, he is a current minister of the Body of Christ in New Mexico.** First however, let me describe something that I have never observed in a real-life minister. With very few exceptions, this minister on each Lord's Day will tell his **congregation** that he will be praying for another local **congregation** and asks them to pray along with him. The **congregation** that he prays for each Lord's Day may be anyone in the community and/or neighboring communities. I must admit my bias of attitude until I read and reread my Bible. **Church** to me is not about **church**! It is all about the **Congregation** of Christians. It is different, but much more meaningful when I occasionally read from the first bit of language that William Tyndale penned that had been used in Koine Greek language.

For example! Let me read to you from a translation completed by Tyndale (A.D. 1525-26), for Jesus, in the Bible from **1ˢᵗ Cor. 16:19. "The congregacions of Asis salute you. Aquilla and Priscilla salute you mouche in the Lorde and so doeth the congregacion that is in their housse."** Christians who meet in their houses for Bible Study are also listening to His words.

My Blessed readers: Would Jesus say, **"You do not go to church! You are the church (ἐκκλησία)! You are Members of the Congregation and/or Assemblies of Christ. And as such, you are called Christians."** Yes, Jesus would say it is just like that. Or like this: **"To be addressed properly, you would be a baptized believer, cognizant of My Father, Myself (Jesus), the Holy Spirit, and much more. You would be living now for the purpose of bringing each member to Spiritual Maturity, as spoken to you in Eph. 4:13."**

Eph. 4:13 Amplified Bible **"[That it might develop] until we all attain oneness in the faith and in the comprehension of the [full and accurate] knowledge of the Son of God, that [we might arrive] at really mature manhood (the completeness of personality which is nothing less than the standard height of Christ's own perfection), the measure of the stature of the fullness of the Christ and the completeness found in Him."**

I think Christ would then say, "And then beloved, knowing that you abide in the above, I recognize each of you as a part of My Congregations of Christ, all being similar in Faith, Duty, and Worship to God, united with the Holy Spirit, regardless if you call yourselves a Baptist, Methodist, Presbyterian, etc., and/or however you choose to abide in My Love, Authority, and the Lord's work, so long that it is in keeping with the scriptures that follow and gain for you a name that gives authority to all Christians as judged by Me (Jesus.)"

Let me provide you information that you can use, connected with Scriptural Reference in **Matt. 28:16-20**. **"Now the eleven disciples went to Galilee, to the mountain to which Jesus had directed and made appointment with them. v17 And when they saw Him, they fell down and worshiped Him; but some doubted. v18 Jesus approached and, breaking the silence, said to them, All Authority (all power of rule) in heaven and on earth has been given to me. v19 Go then and make disciples of all the nations, baptizing them into the name of the Father and of the Son and the Holy Spirit, v20 Teaching them to observe everything that I have commanded you, and behold, I am with you all the days (perpetually, uniformly, and on every occasion) to the [very] close and consummation of the age. Amen (so let it be)."**

Yes, there is a reason in the Call for Uniformity in the One Body of Christ, Worldwide, and for local **congregations**, wherever they may be. His description to us is to be similar, one to the other.

Summary: Words of Life To Help Assist Us To Include The Message!

It is a fact that we have held tightly to words in many Bibles that were not apparently as appropriate as we may have wanted or thought. Every Bible we had in the building, wherever we taught a lesson from the messages of Christ, had the word **church** in it. Yet, we have learned from God's Word in this book using the Koine Greek that Jesus spoke in New Testament times, from translations from William Tyndale, those Biblical words being translated in A.D. 1525-26. The word **church** never entered into the translation. Let's pursue this avenue.

1.   I also believe that these events are rightfully called the Gospel of Jesus Christ our Savior. King James 1st, about 86 years later in A.D. 1611, caused confusion in the world, but it seemed that very few Christians or Biblical Scholars could not do what was needed at that time to prevent a breakdown in what Jesus wanted. Communication efforts were apparently very bad. This move by King James took much of the heart away from the

Christian movement. I believe that the world is only beginning to awaken and understand that King James took it the wrong Direction! Did the King deliberately use the source word Kuriakon, instead of what Jesus apparently wanted, Ekklesia? If he had followed and adhered to the word Ekklesia, as per William Tyndale, this crisis would perhaps have been completely missing in historical development!

2.   As you know, ekklesia translated to either **Assembly** and/or **Congregation**, never to the word **church**. This was the order of the day. If only one checks all the biblical materials to date and makes a note, from perhaps the literature that has been put together in this book, it is my belief that attitudes would quickly translate from "woe and behold", to "Praise William Tyndale's work for Christ!" We are a part of a world with religious leaders who may not see any reason to change to that which Jesus apparently wanted while preaching His word in the first Century, prior to going to be with His Father in Heaven. As I believe and many many others believe, He will return to take the Faithful back with Him to an Eternity of Bliss!

3.   **Matt. 4:4** gives an insight into one matter that Christians continue to ignore, the word of God. Jesus says, **"...man shall not live and be upheld and sustained by bread alone, but by every word that comes forth from the mouth of God."** It seems to me that most men and women professing Christianity from the pulpit in these times, listen to Men and Women more than to The Word of God and Christ! It is one thing to listen to the words of God on all matters of scripture, yet another to those men and often women, that are preaching words to their **congregations** that bear no resemblance to words found in the works of God. It makes it seem that since the time of Jesus' teaching, the Words of God are merrily tossed about for the sake of hearing something different than what is clearly written in the Word.

4.   **Deut. 8:3** reads, **"And He humbled you that He might make you recognize and personally know that man does not live by bread alone, but man lives by every word that proceeds out of the mouth of the Lord."** These same words are essentially recorded above in **Matt. 4:4**

5.   Let's not forget several Scriptures prior to leaving this thought. In **John 5, verses 39, 40, and 44, we find words of learning points that attach to the voice of Jesus Christ. v39** "You search and investigate and pour over the Scripture diligently, because you suppose and trust that you have eternal life through them. And these [very Scriptures] testify about Me! (Jesus) **v40** And still you are not willing [but refuse] to come to Me, so that you might have life." And finally, **v44** states, "How is it possible for you to believe

[how can you learn to believe], you who [are content to seek and] receive praise and honor and glory from one another, and yet do not seek the praise and honor and glory which come from Him Who alone is God?" **Keep An Eye On This!**

6.   **Do not compromise your Biblical training in order to show new attendees that they can change anything they want to change about your Congregation!** Would they or could they? Would it be better to hold the change for a week or two? Hold the change? Yes! What are the thoughts of those who serve the **congregation** as elders? Deacons? Others? Let's take some extra time to study and think it through. Ask yourself and ask your minister what is about to happen within your **congregation** that might bother you? This is literally a stop and think and go again. Keep on track. Keep Jesus with you! Obey God the Father, Our Savior, Jesus the Messiah, and The Holy Spirit.

7.   The Son of God and the Holy Spirit all work directly with one another. For this is the redeeming Power of Eternity that we yearn for, live for and die for, for our beloved leaders in Heaven. We must be ever so conscious of the fact that these Spiritual Beings, through and through, direct us.

8.   His description to us is to be similar, one to the other. Jesus just told us this. My fellow Christians: Jesus the Christ has spoken! We can examine our lives and find exactly where we fall short of the mark, or on the mark! We have received Jesus the King, His Father, and the Holy Spirit. To find if we fall short, or on the mark, takes a great deal of inner strength! The search will be worth it! What would things have looked like today had King James 1st not torn the material asunder in the translation by William Tyndale and replaced it by an unwanted word from another time in this, God's World? The word was **church** and about 86 years later, King James 1st decided to get some translators to change the word from Ekklesia.

The King deliberately used the source word, Kuriakon instead of what Jesus apparently wanted, Ekklesia. And ἐκκλησία (ekklesia) translates to either (**Assembly** and/or **Congregation**), while Kuriakon translates to **church**! This would have been about 675 B.C., prior to Christ's birth as a human to transform the world. Now one might say, "Oh, don't be bothered by such a small change. It fits right in with all the Churches in the land! Jesus wanted this, so don't be so upset. Enjoy it!" If you enjoy it, then whoa!

Many people, many of God's people happen to strongly believe the second to last sentence above, and I am compelled to reply somewhat negatively! As I read the

Bible, Jesus did not want anything other than what He had left planted with Tyndale for the printing press, thus the World. It was a great work, as Tyndale completed the translation that gave us **Congregation** and/or **Assembly**, thus the word ἐκκλησία. This stood the test of time for approximately 86 years before King James 1st found someone to use the key source for the root word, Kuriakon, a word that ultimately converts to the word **church** in English! **So the King got his way!** Let us not be fooled, but I can tell you that I believe the King made a fool of himself. God forgive me if I be wrong! I do think that We need much time in sifting out what constitutes Jesus' wishes!

Your Choice must be God's Choice. Otherwise, we are rapidly confronted by **Col. 2:23, Self-Will Worshipers Choice.** Many are inclined to unknowingly follow in the path of verse 23, yet God's choice remains the one and only choice. Those who are inclined to follow verse 23 should first acquaint themselves with **verse 22**, which says, **"Referring to things all of which perish with being used. To do this is to follow human precepts and doctrines."**[11] Wow! The above words from Christ sound less than preferable to me! **v23 "Such [practices] have indeed the outward appearance [that popularly passes] for wisdom, in promoting self-imposed rigor of devotion and delight in self-humiliation and severity of discipline of the body, but they are of no value in checking the indulgence of the flesh (the lower nature). [Instead, they do not honor God but serve only to indulge the flesh.]"**

I believe that I have interpreted these things well. Just because you think that something is really neat and draws a wave of participants for a short while to your house of worship, don't draw away from God to serve man in his imagination! Anything that might cause this effect, in my humble opinion, would or could be identified as creating an indulgence of the flesh. In bringing this book to fruition, may I suggest a few more ideas that I strongly believe belong to Jesus Christ.

9.   **Acts 8:3** (Tyndale Bible) "But Saul made havocke of the congregacion entrynge into every housse and drew out bothe man and woman and thrust them into preson." **Interpretation**: Not much needed. Saul threw a fit. Stephen was dying, full of the Holy Spirit, and the saints were waiting and praying for him.

10.   Using two different bibles, which scripture (both are **Acts 16:5**) below would be the least suited in this place and why? Consider this time and place to have been in or around Oxford, England in a date given as 1575.

---

[11] See **Isa. 29:13**

1) "So the churches were strengthened and made firm in the Faith, and they increased in number day after day."

2) "So the congregacions stablisshed in the fayth and increased in noumbre dayly."

Answer: This date in no way was 1575! Why? The word **church** existed in The Roman Empire about 2250 years prior to this time, but it was nowhere in the lands of England.

There are two dates we recall if needed in further discussion someday. Translation by Tyndale of his Old and New Testament was A.D. 1525-26 while the new **church** and King James' wild talk arrived in 1611.

11.   Rom. 16:1 "Now I commode vnto you Phebe oure sister (which is a minister of the congregacion) (of the Christians at her house) of Chenchre." We may be sure that Phebe oure sister, ministered to the group of Christians at her house, but it's somewhat doubtful that she preached the Word of God from a pulpit, as we would reckon might be the case in many instances today. I believe she would minister to the ill, take care of Children, help prepare the meals, and everything else that Christ might direct her to do. What kind of service do you think we might experience in a Congregacion of Christ? **Below, I document an actual recent session of worship with Christians in a Ruidoso, New Mexico congregation.**

12.   It was a Sunday Morning Worship Service. Brother Harrell was asked this Day to offer the Communion thoughts during the Lord's Supper. What you read is that which was spoken to about 200 Christians! "Good Morning: We meet together this morning as Brothers and Sisters in Christ in this **Congregation** of Christians. If you are a member of a **congregation** of Christians and are visiting with us today, we ask that you partake in this Lord's Supper with all who are regularly assembled. It is surely good to have you in attendance and we invite you back at your earliest convenience. I believe that Jesus is with us today, as well as each Lord's Day, and that He will hear our expressions, as we Go to God in Prayer for the Bread in our Remembrance of the death of Jesus. We are so very grateful to be called a **congregation** of Christians. We desire to continue to do Your work and offer Praise in your Name for this Bread in commemoration of this celebration. God, we thank you for your son Jesus who died upon the cross to provide us a great opportunity to spend Eternity with all the Saints who will be a part of the Eternal **congregation**. Our Savior will lead us to words that we need so often to invite others to learn of You and Your Son Jesus, the Messiah, whose Body upon the Cross is now remembered by unleavened bread, upon the first day of every week. Accept our deeply seated thanks. It is **in Jesus' name that we pray, Amen!"**

Now if He were with us in person, He might even stand before us and say to this group, "You are the **Congregation** of Christ, as translated by William Tyndale in A.D. 1525-26, for Me, the Messiah." He might wish to recite Acts 11:26, as it was in the form of the Bible at the time mentioned above. It was printed in Ole English and reads as follows:

Acts 11:26 is from a portion of Jesus' remarks, translated by Tyndale from Koine Greek to indicate what this might have sounded like upon its reading! **"And when he had found him, he brought him back vnto Antioche. And it be yt a whole yere chaused and their conversacion with the congregacion so there and had taught mouche people: in that the diciples of Antioch were the fyrst that were called Christen."**

Continuing with the Prayer for Communion: "As a part of this Holy Service on the first day of every week, let's bow our heads and hearts as we remember our Savior. **Dear God**, Thank you for your meaningful and extremely beautiful Day of Remembrance of your Son Who died for our Sins! Continue to cleanse our hearts and help us leave behind us no desire for sin. Help us God as we struggle to live forever and ever with you, Jesus the Christ, the Holy Spirit, our fellow Christians, and our Families. In the memory of Jesus Christ, with this fruit of the vine which represents His blood shed for us, we dedicate our lives anew to Him and Trust Him completely! **In His name we pray, Amen!"**

Address to worshipers: "This is the closing of our communion process! And at this time, not a part of the Lord's Supper. We go to our God and Christ to offer thanks for Giving of our means to those who are very needy! Our Dear Heavenly Father! We approach You at this special time, not a part of our Lord's Supper, yet set aside for giving to those visitors, or our own who may be in dire need of assistance or information concerning God's Holy Word. Holy Father, it is in the Name of Christ Jesus, Your Son, that we offer our prayers and ask that you will continue to lead us to do your Will completely! In His Name we pray, Amen!"

13. Let's review a very meaningful part of the **Bible (Tyndale)** in **1st Cor. 7:17,** which says, "but even as God has **distributed** to every man. As **the Lord hath called** every person so let him walke: and so orden I in all congregacions." Even more significant or perhaps equally so, is a passage of scripture that many Christians in my opinion are beginning to overlook, this one being in **1st Cor. 7:19** "... [but what Counts is] keeping the

Commandments of God!" **This to me is an extremely important statement**. Let nothing get in our way to obey every Commandment. In **1ˢᵗ Cor. 16:19** "The **Congregacions** of Asia salute you. Aquila and Priscilla salute you mouche in the Lord and so doeth those who are meeting in your housse."

For those of you who have a your own copy of this book, please use it to your total benefit as much as you can and stay in tune with The Spiritual episodes of Life and forever an Eternity of Happiness! Once you have found it, never let it go! And once you are with them, you will never go! The most important way to begin to conclude this book is to use a few words that have great meaning for all readers.

First, we have been reminded that each Congregation of Christ **Stands On Its Own**, as a part of God's World. We have learned that a **Congregation** and/or an **Assembly** is preferable in worshiping God, honoring Jesus Christ, and keeping the Holy Spirit with us, rather than a formal **church**, laden with millions of dollars! God, Christ, and the Holy Spirit wish to build us into constant worshipers of Theirs. They desire to have us with them forever and ever! And thus, we desire to be with them, with other Christians, and with Family forever and ever! We will sing with the angels and talk with James, Peter, Luke, John, and all the rest.

We will forever live without sin, enjoy the words of Christian Love and be doing things to keep our love, thoughts, and our very beings in tune with God the Father, Jesus the Messiah, and The Holy Spirit! And always we should enjoy our families! Just think. We will be a part of the Father-God, a member of the Body of Christ, the Messiah and our Savior, and honor and be able to thank the Holy Spirit for His help from time to time!

We must learn to get along with every Christian type, for many of us have shown too much disrespect for some of our people who perhaps did not worship just as we did. If they feel like they need to teach us to do exactly as they do, then it may be time to show more love toward them and show it as a true gesture on our part, as we humble ourselves.

Here is what we perhaps should be working on. One **congregation** proclaims loudly that there be no instrumental music in the worship service. Another one disagrees. A dispute breaks out among the two **congregations**. Both sides seem so angry. What to do? Each side should be ashamed! Each side should stop and take prayers to Jesus and describe the great calamity. We know very well that this is one way to solve a problem. One question. Is it the right way? Let's work on the problem

Together. These two **congregations** are considering to merge into one. Minister (A) has instrumental music in his services, while Minister (B) has no instruments in his a cappella **congregation** of singers.

Chapter Nine

Random And Planned Thoughts Toward Heaven

Minister (A) and Minister (B) have been great leaders of their **congregations**! They have prayed side by side in real efforts to get the two **congregations** to work together in reaching a logical conclusion that both may agree to! Minister (A) and Minister (B) are team players that will try to get these two fine groups to come to an understanding about this current global topic that cannot be easily solved. Minister (A) worships with instrumental music! Minister (B) believes this is not scriptural!

Minister (B) says to Minister (A), "You know that I know that people in your **congregation** are playing instruments when they are singing. Did God and Jesus approve? No! No! Do you not remember that God never wrote on any tablet to give any evidence that makes us believe the Bible calls for songs that are from instrumental music during these present seasons awaiting the Coming of Christ? This music prepares us for the Season of Christ? To do what? Play musical instruments in Heaven? I cannot say you are wrong, because God did not give me discernment about this issue, nor I imagine to you!"

Minister (A) speaks, "Now wait a minute Minister (B). You make a big-to-do thing about this musical instrumental business. Where does it say that we should not use instrumental music in our worship services?"

Minister (B) replies, "Jesus Christ, Son of our most precious God, just might answer this for both of us when we see Him in Heaven!"

Minister (A) says, "Wait, that means when we get to Heaven, we will probably need a unanimous decision or a very good story that will sound like neither of us could make an honest decision."

And then the two ministers engaged in this topic suddenly made a decision! How? No one knows! In about 30 days, Minister (A) and Minister (B) met together with several of their members who knew that this would be a decision day. As you might imagine, this is almost a true story. It shows one of their best efforts and most of all, it's like a true story from God's Word.

The members had patiently waited. Then through the leaves of best kept trees, they heard soft voices! It was those of Minister (A) and Minister (B) combined. They had disguised their voices in neutrality and no one knows who will be talking first. They planned to do it this way! Members could barely distinguish who was who until a strong shout echoed through the large trees and one of the speakers soon would know who would be supporting what, and who would be attentive or disrespectful.

Harnessed voices suddenly began to ring through the air. It seems that the two respected individuals were ready to tell all listeners about their debates, if any, or what the news would be, if any. Approximately 50 people (25 from each **congregation**) were on hand to listen and understand what was being said, be it good, bad, or indifferent! The rules for this great event were these. Minister (A) and Minister (B) now possess the same sounding voices! They will each take the necessary time to get the facts across to their **congregations**! (Story not true yet, but Nearly).

"Good Morning! It is a great day to discuss what we have been saying to one another while generally being civil and trying to see who might come up with the Best Direction as relates to the question of singing with or without instrumental music. Our **congregations** strive for that which will allow for Christian growth. If we were asked this morning to name one thing above all others that would create growth at both of our **congregations**, we would say Unity. Unity means Oneness! To be unified is to be united in Thought, Purpose, Spirit, and Action. The Integrity, Honesty, and Sincerity of each individual must be beyond reproach in order for Harmony and Unity to exist. One of the two, either Minister (A) or Minister (B) pulled out a Bible where they were standing behind what looked like a horse tank, surrounded by fall like leaves in the changing season. And one of the men started talking, but we know not which one. He said, "Folks, I would like to read this Bible that I hold in my hand. We Know that it has real messages for all. I will read ten scriptures, starting with #10 and making my way to #1."

(#10) 1st Cor. 7:19 "For circumcision is nothing and counts for nothing, neither does non-circumcision, but [what counts is] keeping the commandments of God."

Then without saying a word for just a moment, he said, "Listen my friends. This is a serious time," and he began to read from the Book of Acts.

(#9) Acts 18:8 "But Crispus, the leader of the synagogue, believed [that Jesus is the Messiah and acknowledged Him with joyful trust as Savior and/or Lord], together with His entire household; and many of the Corinthians who listened [to Paul also] believed and were baptized."

(#8) John 17:20-21, 26 "Neither for these alone do I pray [it is for their sake only that I make this request], but also all of those who will ever come to believe in (trust in, cling to, rely on) Me through their word and teaching, **v21** That they all may be one, [just] as You, Father, are in Me and I in You, that they also may be one in Us, so that the world may believe and be convinced that You have sent Me." Now read verse 26 and see how it fits in with blessings, both to Jesus and our Heavenly Father. **v26** "and I have made Your name known to them, and will continue to make it known, so that the love with which You have loved Me may be in them [overwhelming their heart], and I [may be] in them."

(#7) Rom. 14:19 "So let us then definitely aim for and eagerly pursue what makes for harmony and for mutual up-building (edification and development) of one another."

Immediately, a majority of listeners from both of these **congregations** let out a yell of blissful joy that could be heard by many farmers in the fields around this wooded area. Likewise, those who hadn't yet shared in this blissful joy kept on talking, but there was evidence of cohesion. Which way did it lean toward? Instrumental music or A Cappella?

(#6) Rom. 15:5-6 "Now may the God Who gives the power of patient endurance (steadfastness) and Who supplies encouragement, grant you to live in such mutual harmony and such full sympathy with one another, in accord with Christ Jesus. **v6** That together you may [unanimously] with united hearts and one voice, praise and glorify the God and Father of our Lord Jesus Christ (the Messiah)."

(#5) Rom. 16:16-18 "Greet one another with a Holy (consecrated) kiss. All the (congregacions) of Christ (the Messiah) wish to be remembered to you. **v17** I appeal to you, brethren, to be on your guard concerning those who create dissensions and difficulties and cause divisions, in opposition to the doctrine (the teaching) which you have been taught. [I warn you to turn aside from them, to] avoid them. **v18** For such persons do not serve our Lord Christ but their own appetites and base desires, and by ingratiating and flattering speech, they beguile the hearts of the unsuspecting and simpleminded [people]."

(#4) 1ˢᵗ Cor. 1:10 "But I urge and entreat you brethren, by the name of our Lord Jesus Christ, that all of you be in perfect harmony and full agreement in what you say, and that there be no dissensions or factions or divisions among you, but that you be **perfectly united in your common understanding** and in your opinions and judgments."

The minister looked at both groups and said, "This verse is an extremely clear and powerful statement from the Apostle Paul for members of both **congregacion**s, to ascertain Differences of Opinion within our two Christian-Centered groups." All listeners were quiet as mice **and we know intuitively, that there is now** tremendous pressure within the thought machines that God gave mankind to use. I also strongly believe that the Apostle Paul had the words exactly correct.

(#3) **2ⁿᵈ Cor. 13:11** "Finally, brethren, farewell (rejoice)! Be strengthened, (perfected, completed, made what you ought to be); be encouraged and consoled and comforted; be of the same [agreeable] mind one with another; live in peace, and [then] the God of Love [Who is the Source of affection, goodwill, love, and benevolence toward men] and the Author and Promoter of peace will be with you."

(#2) **Eph. 4:1-6** "I Therefore, the prisoner for the Lord, appeal to and beg you to walk (lead a life) worthy of the [divine] calling to which you have been called [with behavior that is a credit to the summons to God's service, **v2** Living as becomes you] with complete lowliness of mind (humility) and meekness (unselfishness, gentleness, mildness), with patience, bearing with one another and making allowances because you love one another. **v3** Be eager and strive earnestly to guard and keep the harmony and oneness of [and produced by] the Spirit in the binding power of peace. **v4** [There is] one body and one Spirit--just as there is also one hope [that belongs] to the calling you received-- **v5** [There is] one Lord, one faith, one baptism, **v6** One God and Father of [us] all, Who is above all [Sovereign over all], pervading all and [living] in [us] all."

(#1) **John 14:15** "If you [really] love Me, you will keep (obey) My commands."

Minister (A) and Minister (B) just had their makeup and expensive suits removed by the Word of God, now humbled by what was just read and how it has moved them closer to Jesus and God, also resulting in them being very hesitant to say anything more. Onlookers took their time to say "Well done" to Minister (A) and Minister (B). Will we be able to say who said what? The answer! What was said by Minister (A)? Nothing discernible. What was said by Minister (B)? Nothing discernible. **Nothing discernible after all that?** Remember, both voices were disguised.

Eternal Victory Ranking below from #1 to #10

The Paved Lane for Achievement and Victory provides key points for those who are seeking The Scripture and Words For Everlasting Life!

Keys To Heaven And Eternal Life

1.	John 14:15	If you really love me, keep my Commandments
2.	Eph. 4:1-6	One Lord - One Faith - One Baptism
3.	2nd Cor. 13:11	Be with the same agreeable mind, in Peace
4.	1st Cor. 1:10	Let there be no divisions; be United in opinion
5.	Rom. 16:16-17	Be on your guard; let no one mislead you
6.	Rom. 15:5-6	God grant us perfect harmony, united hearts
7.	Rom. 14:19	Pursue eagerly what makes Harmony
8.	John 17:20-21, 26	Trust Jesus in Word and Teaching
9.	Acts 18:8	Savior & Lord, many believed – were saved
10.	1st Cor. 7:19	Circumcision? No - Commandments of God? Yes

The previous ten Biblical locations of scripture will be transformed into the final actions below, leading toward what I think the God-Head will be addressing per the musical instrument question/decision.

(1)   John 14:15 "If you [really] love Me, you will keep (obey) My commands."

Jesus is speaking very graciously and will continue His verbiage for each one listening to Him who will keep his/her willingness to Keep and (Obey) His Commandments. The validity of the True Christ is our complete validity of Obedience to the True Savior, and always true and honest toward the love that we have promised the Savior!

(2)   Eph. 4:1-6 "I Therefore, the prisoner for the Lord, appeal to and beg you to walk (lead a life) worthy of the [divine] calling to which you have been called [with behavior that is a credit to the summons to God's service. v2 Living as becomes you] with complete lowliness of mind (humility) and meekness (unselfishness, gentleness, mildness), with patience, bearing with one another and making allowances because you love one another. v3 Be eager and strive earnestly to guard and keep the harmony and oneness of [and produced by] the Spirit in the binding power of peace. v4 [There is] one body and one Spirit--just as there is also one hope [that belongs] to the calling you received. v5 [There is] one Lord, one faith, one baptism, v6 One God and Father of [us] all, Who is above all [Sovereign over all], pervading all and [living] in [us] all."

One might preach a complete sermon many times using this material written by Paul. Notice in these scriptures he emphasizes Living as He would have us live, namely complete lowliness of mind (humility) and meekness (**unselfishness, gentleness, mildness**), with patience, bearing with one another and making allowances because you love one another. These three words in bold print are tremendous power for us to possess. Power to give, power to yield, and Power to Love, as we treat people like we would want them to treat us!

(3)   2ⁿᵈ Cor. 13:11 "Finally, brethren, farewell (rejoice)! Be strengthened (perfected, completed, made what you ought to be), be encouraged and consoled and comforted, be of the same [agreeable] mind one with another, live in peace, and [then] the God of Love [who is the source of affection, goodwill, love, and benevolence toward men] and the Author and Promoter of peace will be with you."

(4)   1ˢᵗ Cor. 1:10 "But I urge and entreat you brethren, by the name of our Lord Jesus Christ, that all of you be in perfect harmony and full agreement in what you say, and that there is no dissensions or factions or divisions among you, but that you be perfectly united in your common understanding and in your opinions and judgments."

This, brethren, is one that we have been waiting for! It suggests to me and many others to give it a second thought. We have lived with our Christian brothers and sisters for many years. Some are remarkably adapted to listen, analyze, and go forward to victory. Others wait and see which side they should take. It can't be said any better than in the AMP Bible. The Apostle Paul said what he wanted to say without hesitation. His story is short and his message is absolutely miraculous, to the point, and can be used in almost any situation involving decision making. Life in many ways is constant decision making isn't it? **Verse 10** is beautifully stated and I would hope that I can make a point without ruining, in any way, my intention! We have just witnessed in this verse a Voice from on High saying, "**Live in perfect harmony.**" How do we do such a thing? We add the words, "**and full agreement**" in what we say, and then do those biblical things that we are told to do in this verse! What does this produce? **No dissensions or factions or divisions among us**. This allows us to be perfectly united in our common understanding and in our opinions and judgments.

Watch For Trouble--This Is Where It May Begin

(5)   Rom. 16:16-18 "Greet one another with a Holy (consecrated) kiss. All the churches[12] of Christ (the Messiah) wish to be remembered to you. **v17** I appeal to you, brethren, those who create dissensions and difficulties and those who cause divisions, in oppositions to the doctrine (the teaching) which you have been taught. [I warn you to turn aside from them, to] avoid them. **v18** For such persons do not serve our Lord Christ but their own appetites and base desires, and by ingratiating and flattering speech, they beguile the hearts of the unsuspecting and simpleminded [people]."

This Is What Must Be Watched Like A Hawk

As the Body of Christ, if we wish to continue to keep pace in thinking about maintaining a healthy Body of Christ with minimal outside interference, we need more thought and guidance from Heaven.

(6)   Rom. 15:5-6 "Now may the God Who gives the power of patient endurance (steadfastness) and Who supplies encouragement, grant you to live in such mutual harmony and such full sympathy with one another, in accord with Christ Jesus. **v6** That together you may [unanimously] with united hearts and one voice, praise and glorify the God and Father of our Lord Jesus Christ (the Messiah)."

Again, the Apostle Paul is writing for the Heaven and the Earth! Notice God's identity of people: Steadfastness, encouragement, mutual harmony and full sympathy with one another in accord with Jesus Christ. **Verse 6** gives us a real vision for what is to become. "That together you may [unanimously] with united hearts and one voice, praise and glorify the God and Father of our Lord Jesus Christ (the Messiah)."

---

[12] Should be **Congregations** and/or **Assemblies**

(7)   Rom. 14:19 "So let us then definitely aim for and eagerly pursue what makes for harmony and for mutual upbuilding (edification and development) of one another."

Harmony, edification, and development! (Mutual Upbuilding). Not a better use of words could be found. On target!

(8)   John 17:20-21, 26 "Neither for these alone do I pray [it is not for their sake only that I make this request], but also all of those who will ever come to believe in (trust in, cling to, rely on) Me through their word and teaching, **v21** That they all may be one, [just] as You, Father, are in Me and I in You, that they also may be one in Us, so that the world may believe and be convinced that You have sent Me. **v26** I have made Your name known (God speaking to Jesus) to them (friends and enemies) and revealed your character and your very Self, and I will continue to make [You] known, that the love which You bestowed upon Me may be in them [felt in their hearts] and that I [Myself] may be in them."

This is the ultimate sacrifice and act of love, one that is to be carried out with a Father (God) who knew (Him) Jesus the Messiah, had to be crucified on a cross so that you and I might have Eternal Life. It was to be the MOST victorious event and was completely done for you, me and all the people in the world. The love that Jesus showed us on the cross is absolutely unbelievable!

Having said that, I can also say that I believe that it portrays the Greatest Victory of Mankind! There is no doubt whatsoever! I trust that all who read this will Believe this, Obey this, and Live this daily. It is your Salvation and mine to do so. May God forever bless you and yours!

(9)   Acts 18:8 "But Crispus, the leader of the synagogue, believed [that Jesus is the Messiah and acknowledged Him with joyful trust as Savior and Lord], together with His entire household; and many of the Corinthians who listened [to Paul also] believed and were baptized."

This is just a reminder that these sinners were much like you and me. This happened early in the 1st Century. It occurred because God and His Son cleared the way and opened up the Highway to Heaven and Eternity.

(10)   1st Cor. 7:19 "For circumcision is nothing and counts for nothing, neither does non circumcision, but [what counts is] keeping the commandments of God."

Nothing can be stronger for you, me, other Christians, and all that Read the Bible, Hear the Word, and Ask to become a Christian, than to read and keep on reading the Word of God. Strange as it may be, this thought may indeed begin to work miracles.

You will recall that we left behind our two **congregations** that were discussing the pros and cons of combining their Body of Christians. We referred to our leadership as Minister (A) and Minister (B). We knew that Minister (A) wanted to worship with instrumental music, while Minister (B) had never experienced this before and strongly opposed phasing this in as a part of any possible merge.

It is now time to begin the process of merging these two **congregations** into one. Is this even possible? I revert back to **#4** on my Eternal Victory Ranking list. **1st Cor. 1:10 "But I urge and entreat you brethren, by the name of our Lord Jesus Christ, that all of you be in perfect harmony and full agreement in what you say and that there is no dissensions or factions or divisions among you, but that you be perfectly united in your common understanding and in your opinions and judgments."**

There is something remarkable about this verse. It is beautifully stated and I would hope that I can make a point without ruining, in any way, my intention! We have just witnessed in this verse a Voice from on High saying "be in perfect harmony." How do we do such a thing? We add the words "and full agreement" in what we say, and then do those biblical things that we are told to do in this verse! What does this produce? "No dissensions or factions or divisions among us." This allows us to be "perfectly united in your (our) **common understanding** and in your (our) opinions and judgments."

There is one thing that we should all recognize prior to allowing Minister (A) and Minister (B) to begin their discussion of **To merge two congregations into one or not to merge based on differences in worshiping God through song**. Both **congregations** have many elderly members who have worshiped God and His Son for many many years. This factor of consideration arises from a figure that when this type of change occurs in a **Congregation**, roughly 18% will begin to migrate to other nearby Congregations of Christ and/or start a new **congregation** of their own. Minister (A) and Minister (B) then begin the discussion by first introducing a special guest.

"Brothers and Sisters in Christ! Most of you have met in private with Dr. Roger Harrell concerning matters now at hand. He is a former School Superintendent of 16 years and also served as a Minister for several Bodies of Christ throughout the country, in places he was led to by the various school districts who sought his expertise." And so, Dr. Harrell said, "Thank you. It has been my privilege to have discussed matters at hand with your leaders prior to today, both Ministers (A) and (B) along with several elders from both **congregations**. As you know, your Congregations of Christ have been discussing the possibility of merging into one, as both seek to demonstrate cohesion and unity, thus creating the opportunity for new growth. Your ministers have been very supportive of the ongoing discussions.

May I please ask these two gentlemen to bring you a short report on the plans they have to immediately accomplish three things:

1.) Permit one new consolidated building if the majority of elders and members at each **congregation** are in agreement.

2.) Encourage new thoughts in line with scripture and in line with the building clause.

3.) Assist in every way we can in moving in the direction that we feel is right for both **congregations**.

I would now like to ask Ministers (A) and (B) to visit with you on a critical matter."

Minister (A) decides to speak first. "Good morning everyone! Thank you for your attendance today. Let me begin by placing on this chalkboard, a scripture that is amazing when building an idea, a fishing house on the side of a lake, a plain, comfortable home to raise children or a building to house members of a Congregation of Christ. These words originate from **1ˢᵗ Cor. 1:10** and I now take a moment to show what may cause the pursuit of the whole idea to be set aside for time to reconsider or hit the road running!" **1ˢᵗ Cor. 1:10**: "But I urge and entreat you brethren, by the name of our Lord Jesus Christ, that all of you *be in perfect harmony, in full agreement, no dissensions or factions or divisions among us, perfectly united in your common understanding, and in your opinions and judgments.*"

Minister (A) continues, "And now let's italicize the first part of the scripture, words that are **Seeking a Way**: *But I urge and entreat you brethren, by the name of our Lord Jesus Christ, that all of you …*"

And so we have a message from the Apostle who wrote this, that we may know of

God's wishes and that he, the Apostle Paul calls to our attention, that which was going on in Corinth, where apparently the rich and famous brought sin of sins to the people who lived there or to those who made elongated visits for the purpose of sin. This sounds very much the same as the Halls of Fun. Think they are? No, not yet. What duds, what shame, and what a slam to what the Body of Jesus Christ was/is all about.

Shortly thereafter, Minister (B) picked up where Minister (A) left off. He whistled loudly and the chatter came to a halt. He began by saying, "Please let me have your attention! We have a problem that you must help us solve. The issue was clearly stated by Minister (A), but first by God and His Son Jesus Christ. We had our good brother Paul vividly write scripture that basically has us thinking and wondering what we should do. Listen again and tell us what you think we should do based on your understanding."

"But I urge and entreat you brethren, by the name of our Lord Jesus Christ, that all of you be in perfect harmony, and full agreement, in what you say, and that there be no dissensions, or factions or divisions among you, but that you, be perfectly united in our common understanding, and in our opinions and judgments."

One of Minister (B)'s members yelled out, "Is this the real picture of thinking of this group?" Minister (B) was a bit shaken when he heard this comment. Minister (A) and his wife could hardly speak. They both looked at Dr. Harrell, with Minister (A) saying, "We're glad that you came our way. My wife and I must admit that we have had instrumental music so long in our **congregation** that right now, we have no business taking on change. We are certainly not suited for the changes we've been discussing."

Dr. Harrell replied, "Are there any members of your **congregation** who disagree with you?" Minister (A) stated, "There are several, perhaps as many as five families who vehemently said NO to us concerning the merge." Dr. Harrell asked, "And what reason would you be able to give God or Christ in saying that five families didn't want to go through with the merger of these two Congregations of Christ?"

After participating in some of the discussion, Dr. Harrell could tell that both **congregations** had a big looming problem. It all had to do with two different ways of singing praises to God. Minister (A) wished to continue with instrumental music and Minister (B) felt there was no other scriptural proof in singing with instruments and acknowledging that many **congregations** have turned into rock concerts.

With discussions taking a rapid turn for the worse, Harrell felt there was still a way that disagreements could be worked out. He immediately got the attention of the crowd by slightly raising his voice and asking, **"Can anyone describe what these two congregations are all about?"**

One elderly gentleman raised his hand and said in a loud voice to all of the people, "What we have here today are two **congregations** that have not matured in Christ Jesus. Why don't we listen to the wisdom of others who are here today?" Then an older man who was hunched over with a troubled back stepped forward and read from scripture that had been previously focused on. "But I urge and entreat you brethren, by the name of our Lord Jesus Christ, that all of you be in perfect harmony, and full agreement, (with) no dissensions, or factions or divisions among us, perfectly united in your common understanding, and in your opinions and adjustments."

If in your mind it sounds as though tensions are rising, you would be correct. The hunched over man asked for and received one more opportunity to address his fellow Christians. He said with a nervous shiver, "My good friends. Not all of us sound a bit insane and we are truly a good people. I have known many of you for more than 40 or 50 years. Today's discussion is not all lost and we need to take the bull by the horns to begin straightening ourselves out on the subject of how we worship God in song. We should ask ourselves, **Did God authorize us to use instrumental music?"**

Dr. Harrell stepped forward and concluded with his mediation by saying, "I must admit that I have searched far and wide for this answer for the last 65 years and to date, I haven't found one. But you know what? We can search until we leave this life for eternity. God will help us sing with instruments if He really meant for us to do so."

Minister (A) turned to Dr Harrell, thanked him for his participation and asked him to lead both **congregations** in prayer. Harrell asked everyone to bow with him and boldly prayed the following:

"Our Holy Father in Heaven. Thank you so much for the love of your Children, for everyone standing here with their heads bowed. We beseech you for Wisdom in learning and forever knowing 1st Cor. 1:10, a powerful verse that you placed in your Bible of Wisdom. We call upon You to help each of us to know the Wisdom of Knowing You, Oh God. Thank You God for the way that you have helped us begin to search, day and night, for the Wisdom that you bring to each of us in our weakness. We now know, Father, how we became so loved by you and our Christ Jesus, that being full recognition of the powers You have, and those that have become yours who wear the garments of Christianity. These garments have begun to fit us better for strife that we meet head-on, and for wisdom that you have shared with us to do your work in keeping with your directions of living a more perfect life. Thank you God for showing us a better way through actions in 1st Cor. 10. In the name of Jesus our Savior, Amen!"

After praying, Dr. Harrell visited for a short time, yet long enough for many of the assembled to share their appreciation of him for his concern and Godly advice.

What impresses me so much about 1st Cor. 1:10 is the thought that no one else besides God, Jesus, and the Holy Spirit, knew what was really being said. Words that they used below were at one time known only by the Three and whomever else was granted the privilege of knowing that they were words dealing with the attitude of God's people. For my sake and yours, I want to record them one more time prior to bringing closure. **1st Cor. 1:10** in the Amplified Topical Reference Bible reads, **"But I urge and entreat you, brethren, by the name of our Lord Jesus Christ, that all of you be in perfect harmony and full agreement in what you say, and that there be no dissensions or factions or divisions among you, but that you be perfectly united in your common understanding and in your opinions and judgments."**

These words are words to live by and die by and to talk about when we all get to Heaven! They send shivers through my body. They will be with me as long as I live and will guide me to love God, Jesus Christ, and the Holy Spirit. They continue what is my perception of the love of my family (my wife, my children, my grandchildren) and friends until the very end.

We've spent a great deal of time on 1st Cor. 1:10, but now I'd like to look at the very next verse, which says, **v11** "For it has been made clear to me, my brethren, by those of Chloe's household, that there are contentions and wrangling and factions among you." This was Paul's problem and I am sure he received Godly information that provided help to separate the two groups in verse 11, especially from what is made known in Part 1 just ahead. Without verse 11, we run the risk of missing the point that Jesus makes! You will remember this as will other readers!

Part I of 1st Cor. 1:10: "But I urge and entreat you, brethren, by the name of our Lord Jesus Christ, that all of you be in perfect harmony and full agreement in what you say, and that there be no dissensions or factions or divisions among you,"

Part II of 1st Cor. 1:10: If only reading the second part of verse 10, it's a bit different from the first part, saying, "but that you be perfectly united in your common understanding and in your opinions and judgments." Let's make this more clearly understood by adding verse 11, which lends itself to Part I.

Part III: 1ˢᵗ **Cor. 1:11** (Paul still speaking), "For it has been made clear to me, my brethren, by those of Chloe's household, that there are contentions and wrangling and factions among you." When this verse appears, things begin to get situated correctly in the mind of man!

Clarification of Parts I, II, and III

Part I above finds the Apostle Paul urging the brethren in Corinth to be in perfect harmony and full agreement, and once you get this agreement in the minds of all members of the **Congregation** in Corinth, you will no longer find dissensions or factions or divisions among you. This is a very good start.

Part II: Now still in verse 10, it says that you are to be perfectly united in your common understanding and in your opinions and judgments. Whoa! Something went wrong. Instead of really answering Part I with his first intentions, Paul uses "judgments" that undoubtedly is embarrassing for many.

Part III: Paul quickly communicated in no uncertain terms with a reply to Part I and Part II, saying in verse 11, "For it has been made clear to me, my brethren, by those of Chloe's household, that there are contentions and wrangling, and factions among you." Not Paul's thoughts till now, but he clearly knows that the situation is likely to erupt at any time, thus leaving a stern message for worshipers.

I sincerely hope for reasons of learning and teaching that you may figure out ways to properly use this material in a manner that reflects the true desire of Jesus.

Briefly: William Tyndale developed the basic material that he had in Koine Greek from our Christ Jesus in order to fulfill the request to make sure that when printed, all would be able to enjoy beautiful encounters of Tyndale's printing of the Old English Language. Consequently, the benefit of requested language that was translated in Old English resulted in many true words, such as **Congregations** instead of **Churches**, and/or **Assembly** instead of **church**. With all of my heart, I know this is what Jesus wanted--a **Congregation** or an **Assembly** of Christians instead of a **church**. Tyndale's correctly translated Bible appeared in 1525-26 A.D. and King James 1ˢᵗ later threw a fit, wanting a version of the word **church** from about 2,250 years prior and in another language. Did the King conclude that they could sell a different printing of this book? Yes, as he was able to sell a concept to people he was in charge of. He wanted to call this book the Bible, as it had been called, and is still being called. He could get away with it by doing this and he would succeed. He would use an incorrect language and he would get what he wanted, words that meant something entirely different than their original intention. Words that would not be a threat to him and others in positions of power. And what happened? He got away with it!

The King James Bible - Authorized Version was dated 1611. This means that King James 1st was able to get his Bible printed 86 years after Tyndale's Biblical Translation, virtually halting the printing of Tyndale's correctly translated Bible. Tyndale was murdered on Oct. 6th, 1536, strangled and then burned at the stake. His last words occurred after he was tried and ridiculously convicted for heresy and treason. Those words were, "Lord, open the King of England's eyes."

Many authors who have studied the differences in material written by Tyndale and subsequently used by King James 1st are prone to utter such things as, "About 70% to 80% of the material in King James' Bible sounds very much like Tyndale's work."

Chapter Ten

A Look At The Praise And Care Of Christians

My thanks to those who have biblical knowledge about this content and will at the same time be thinking as I, "How can we do things differently that are a necessity, but have neither the money nor the time?" We can continue to read, listen, and take prayerful action. However, let me first say that many of our Christian people should be called "Members of the Congregation of Christ."

That which perhaps might be the most appropriate response could be to continue to pray and ask that God, Christ, and the Holy Spirit guide each of us to those things that may tend to bring victory through Prayer, to individuals such as we, to help us grow, to know better what we may do for this cause. It will take great patience, consistent prayer, and a constant longing to be of help to those who do not yet know the what and why of King James' takeover of something so precious as the word of Jesus Christ.

When we dove into scripture from my Eternal Victory Ranking list, we read about multiple qualities that we can use as helpful information throughout our journey as a Christian. This lifetime of useable knowledge paves a lane for achievement and victory, as eternal life is within our grasp. These scriptures contain the substance necessary for getting one's life together. Notice that (#1) is essentially the same as (#10). This my friends leads us to Heaven and Eternity!

(#1) John 14:15 "If you [really] love Me, you will keep (obey) my Commands."

(#10) 1st Cor. 7:19 "For circumcision is nothing and counts for nothing, neither does non circumcision, but [what counts is] keeping the commandments of God."

These ten vital points lead to patterns that we should learn to Live by, as our remaining years slip from us and are tended by God, Jesus, and the Holy Spirit. Not only should we lead others to Godly patterns that we are trying to live by, but it is imperative that we teach others as we have occasions to do so.

Taking Action In Obeying Our Lord Jesus and Keeping The Peace

If we were asked today to name one thing above all others that would cause growth of Character and Maturity at our Congregations of Christ, I would say Unity. Unity means Oneness! It means no dissensions! To be unified is to be united in Thought, Purpose, Spirit, and Action. The Integrity, Honesty, and Sincerity of each individual must be beyond reproach in order for Harmony and Unity to Exist. Unity is following the words of Christ for Peace and Harmony and all ingredients that should be incorporated in the words we have been reading!

However, there are many times that Jesus and His workers fill the air around us with caution. For example, listen to the Apostle Paul as he gives comfort, and appeals to his brethren in **Rom. 16:17.** He said, **"I appeal to you, brethren, to be on your guard concerning those who create dissensions and difficulties and cause divisions, in opposition to the doctrine (the teaching) which you have been taught. [I warn you to turn aside from them, to] avoid them."**

As you begin to find reasons of certainty in each of the ten points encountered in the preceding pages, I believe strongly that you are finding new and exciting material. As we draw closer to Christ, I believe that we will make a concerted effort to carry with us at all times, the material of Christianity, Honesty, Truthfulness in Heart, and Discernment as to Right vs. Wrong, able to carry the burdens when of Right. In these moments, God, Jesus, and the Holy Spirit are at work to give all true Christian brothers and sisters a Blessed Home for Eternity!

Let's examine two critical points that are within our grasp. We have mentioned them in passing, but not to the extent that is needed! As we know, there are several things that may be wrong about us in what we do while we live as Christians in this world. I have never met a person who is a scholar of Biblical Studies to say that it was incorrect for William Tyndale to put into World circulation, the Word of God that was given to him to translate from Koine Greek to English for publication in the form of Bibles. He translated biblical material for both New and Old Testaments. I've already told you that story, but I haven't shared with you this part of the story! Think about it and Pray about it! What we can and will say is the truth.

Point #1: I believe that Jesus did everything He was called to do from the time of His birth until He was crucified. He was able to indirectly place material into the hands of William Tyndale, work that had been completed in the early days of the Apostles, to be used in printed Bibles for teaching about Heaven, Hell and Eternal Life in A.D. 1525-26.

Many people today are often disappointed in worship services when they are told that Tyndale had not placed one word in his translation of the Koine Greek to build the word **C_H_U_R_C_H**! He was to use only the Greek word for ekklesia, (ἐκκλησία), and from this word, it could not be translated to any words other than **Assembly** and/or **Congregation**! This excluded the word **church**! The Bible warns us that anyone who destroys or changes The Word could be condemned to destruction!

Point #2: Gal. 1:6-9 was written by the Apostle Paul for Jesus our Savior and says,

v6 "I am surprised and astonished that you are so quickly turning renegade and deserting Him Who invited and called you by the Grace (unmerited favor) of Christ (the Messiah) [and that you are transferring your allegiance] to a different [even an opposition] gospel.

v7 Not that there is [or could be] any other [genuine Gospel] but there are [obviously] some who are troubling and disturbing and bewildering you [with a different kind of teaching which they offer as a gospel] and want to pervert and distort the Gospel of Christ (the Messiah) [into something which it absolutely is not.]

v8 But even if we or an angel from heaven should preach a Gospel contrary to and different from that which we preached to you, let him be accursed (anathema, devoted to destruction, doomed to eternal punishment)!

v9 As we said before, so I now say again: If anyone is preaching to you a gospel different from or contrary to that which you received [from us] let him be accursed (anathema, devoted to destruction, doomed to eternal punishment)!"

Afterthoughts

Someone mentioned above undoubtedly was not listening. Who was that someone? It was he who called himself Great and who answered to the name of King James 1st. You have read his story in this book. You are aware that he was able to get his followers to do all his bidding and changing things such that he was able to get a new Bible processed in His Kingship. You might have a copy of the King James Bible - Authorized Version, dated around A.D. 1611. The Bible that William Tyndale developed for worldwide use had maybe two words that would begin to sound like c—h—u—r—c—h in English and those two referenced Houses of Sin. As I have mentioned several times in this writing, the word **church** was taken from another era of B.C. approximately 2,500-2,800 years ago.

In many places, it was to be the MOST victorious event and was completely done for you, me and everyone on earth. The love that Jesus showed us on the cross is absolutely unbelievable. Having said that, I can also say that I believe that it portrays forever, the Greatest Victory for God, Christ, and the Holy Spirit! There is no doubt whatsoever! I trust that all people who read this will believe this, obey this, and live this daily. It is your salvation and mine to do so. May God forever bless you and yours!

As in most cases today, there seem to be two factions to every internal Congregational proposal concerning change. One faction is part of a group that really wants to change by using a certain amount of unwanted pressure. I believe they become somewhat of an unconscious group when thoughts turn to "How?" and "When?" That leaves another group that wants things to remain as they have been throughout the years. And why? This group has established patterns. After all, they have been worshiping together for about 30 years or so! This once-satisfied group of status quo Christians felt the truth, they lived the truth, and they were the truth.

A Look At What A Few Of The Early Pioneers Had To Say

John Calvin--Presbyterian Congregation

John Wesley--Methodist Congregation

Adam Clarke--Methodist Congregation

Martin Luther--Lutheran Congregation

Charles Spurgeon--Baptist Congregation

What do we have in common with these folks? Let's read and we will quickly find out. We'll identify a few by their actions, thoughts, and productive talk.

a.   **John Calvin (Presbyterian Congregation)** "But when they frequent their sacred assemblies, musical instruments in celebrating the praises of God would be no more suitable than the burning of incense, the lighting up of lamps, and the restoration of the other shadows of the law. The Papists, therefore, have foolishly borrowed this, as well as many other things from the Jews. Men who are fond of outward pomp may delight in that noise; but the simplicity God recommends to saints only, in a known tongue, is (1st Cor. 14:16)." (Portion of Calvin's Commentary[13] on Psalms 33:2)

---

[13] https://www.studylight.org/commentaries/cal/psalms-33.html

b.   John Wesley (Founder of the Methodist Congregation) "I have no objection to instruments of music in our chapels, provided they are neither heard nor seen." (Adam Clarke's Commentary - Vol. 4 pg. 686)

c.   Adam Clarke (Methodist) "I am an old man, and an old minister; and I here declare that I never knew (instruments of music) them productive of any good in the worship of God; and have had reason to believe that they were productive in much evil. Music as a science, I esteem and admire; but instruments of music in the house of God I abominate and abhor. This is the abuse of music; and I register my protest against all such corruptions in the worship of the Author of Christianity." (Adam Clarke's Commentary - Vol. 4 pg. 686)

d.   Martin Luther (Lutheran) "Martin Luther called the organ an ensign of Baal." (McClintock & Strong's Encyclopedia)

e.   Charles Spurgeon (Baptist) "We might as well pray by machinery as praise by it." (The Treasury of David - Psalms 42)

Most of these great leaders would not recognize a worship service today in the buildings they once attended and provided outstanding leadership. However, no one can deny that they tried to continue their worship services without instrumental music.

These folks, these great leaders, were giants in this world at that time. I can only speculate that if they had the opportunity today, they would continue their steadfast battle of trying to maintain the musical instrument as one to be used in places, but not worship.

Gathering Tools And Ideas In Making Fair Decisions For Everyone

One of the toughest things to be done from this point until the end of the book is to show fairness and reasonableness to all. The mindset of those who will be making decisions will be essential to avoid creating chaos. Fairness and reasonableness are absolutely essential.

Any tool chosen by a writer, speaker, or otherwise at this point in the manuscript must have a purpose, and the user of the tool must be willing to abide by its purposeful use! In retrospect, we are aligning readers with planned programs of:

<u>To Do</u> or <u>Not To Do</u>!

The following items must be accounted for in the final choice for securing things that are known to work in obtaining results, as well as recognizing things that we know too often have failed, yet we keep on using them.

Briefly, but purposefully, we want to accomplish What? The Purpose is to set final goals related to bringing to the surface, things that will be needed in order to begin to develop plans and put those plans into action to attain goals that need to be addressed by Congregations of Christians.

Returning to our Ministers (A) and (B) and the decisions each have to make, I truly believe that with this example and many more that you've been exposed to, one can piece together a strategy to become more like Jesus Himself by taking on the character of a person who does not always feel the need for instrumental music in a place such as Minister (B)'s **Assembly** and/or **Congregation**.

To each of these two **congregations** I must say, here are steps to success: Follow the command of our Savior and He will guide you in Praying, Studying, and Listening. And now it is time for me (RLH) to step into the picture again as an outside consultant.

Decision On The Congregations Singing With Instruments Or Without

"**Good Morning Brothers and Sisters!** It is another beautiful day in Ruidoso, New Mexico. It is good to be back in your area, ready to pursue as you have chosen, the avenue of seeking the Favor of Christ in regard to music for the heart and soul of Christians. I have continued to assess those in the field of music, to honor and sing praises to those whom we Love above, God our Creator, Jesus our Savior and King, along with the Holy Spirit who has been in touch with so many of us, even at times when we feel we are not worthy of memory.

Yet as many of us who have worked with all Three and who have fully addressed God's Spiritual Genuineness, we ask for prayer as we ready ourselves to look more deeply and intently toward each of your Congregational wishes, this one in particular regarding music and singing, with or without the use of musical instruments!"

At this point in the book, I wish to cover several issues in dealing with the outcome that may or may not materialize regarding working together to declare what we believe we need to address, as we focus on placing ourselves in positions to outline our goals.

We called our leadership Minister (A) and Minister (B). We knew that Minister (A) wanted to keep instrumental music in his worship services, while Minister (B) had never worshiped with instruments and strongly opposed bringing this to the instructional phase in a change-over/merge. It is now time to continue the quest of integrating the two **congregations** while attempting to fit the mindset of both factions within each **congregation**. Is this even possible? This is the question of the hour!

Someone asked, "Dr. Harrell, will you once again guide us in prayer?" With an affirmative nod, he lowered his head along with everyone else and immediately had thoughts of Jesus, feeling as though He wanted to hear what was being said. Thoughts turned to garments of Christianity fitting us better for strife that we meet head-on and for wisdom that has been shared with us to do His work in keeping with His directions of living a more perfect life. The prayer appropriately ended with, **"Thank you God for showing us a better way through Actions in 1st Cor. 1:10-11 and similar words from our Bibles. In the name of Jesus We Pray, Amen!"**

Dr. Harrell said to the musical instrument and non-musical instrument **congregations**, "Since my last communication with you, I have spoken at length with Minister (A) and Minister (B). Both seem determined to continue conducting their Song Service in the same manner as they have for as long as they can remember. They each also serve as Lead Elder for their **congregation**, if there be such one. Some say they have leaders and others do not. During our most recent conversation, I again began to read what was previously read concerning the scriptural 10 points of truth and victory. Each one has a strength when it comes to keeping the brotherhood in tune with the Word, gently being used to keep the Love that has been talked about so much in the Bible, a part of Christian life! Scripture to me is by far the most reliable method that can be used to take on the personality of Jesus, God, and our frequent Helper, the Holy Spirit! When you read, you will again have reviewed at least the Creativeness of God in keeping folks Happy and Christlike, a Goal of Christ Jesus until problematic issues are resolved. If they are not resolved, God will undoubtedly one day do so."

Almost Decision Time For Both Congregations

1st Cor. 1:10-11 ".... that all of you be in perfect harmony and full agreement in what you say, and that there is no dissensions or factions or divisions among you ...." Paul might then ask, "But have you been honest with me? Have you indeed been (perfectly united in your common understanding, and in your opinions and judgments?") **v11 "For it has been made clear to me, my brethren, by those of Chloe's household, that there**

are contentions and wrangling and factions among you." In this verse, Paul could have said, "You kept a household for those who were getting solid sermons, but there were also those who were divisive and most certainly not united." Wow! Think, Think and Think again! There is a vast quantity of knowledge to be obtained concerning both Wisdom and Discernment from reading the scriptures beyond verse 11. Continue to read and read and read again!

Let's get back to Dr. Harrell, our visiting consultant who's still speaking and is about ready to give instruction to the two **congregations** concerning the difficult decisions they have to make.

"May I advise you that all recommendations that were brought to my attention during the past couple of months, have been studied with much concern for your feelings. The leadership (elders, ministers, board members, teachers) of each **congregation** along with all members will secure a decision via paper ballot at this meeting.

Based upon all the Biblical data that I have seen and shared with you along with the information gained from your respective elders and ministers representing each congregation, I must say to all that my recommendation is to maintain status quo for a period of time!

The one thing that I really thought was missing was the urging from God, Christ, and the Holy Spirit. I felt that each **congregation** was defending the status-quo of their music programs. From the Bible, we heard the voices of Paul, Jesus, the Holy Spirit and the wonderful saturation of words coming from the Trinity above, with admonitions that were at the present time in my thinking of action, not yet suited for a uniting of these two **congregations**. I really could not bring my own feelings, such as they were, to believe that the words in **1ˢᵗ Cor. 1:10-11** were monitored and legitimized by members of each **congregation** to reflect the ingredients of unity, perfect harmony, full agreement in what you say, no dissensions or factions or divisions among you, perfectly united in your common understanding and in your opinions and judgments. That of course was from verse 10 and then when verse 11 was analyzed, I became a solid believer that the two **congregations** are definitely on different tracks! One group felt compelled to keep the truth to itself and made mistakes in what they were doing to bring the kind of maturity to bear the load. And now may I ask, are emotions running high or low or not at all?"

Two Board Members who graciously smiled, raised their hands with one of them saying, "Dr. Harrell, we met with our groups this morning and I think you said what we really wanted to hear today. We need more time to talk to you and other biblical scholars. All of us want to do a lot and we think we know what we intend to do. We are thankful for your guidance and we will touch bases on down the road. We suggest that we continue to talk with our leaders and you about every 3 months and see what might be in the making, if anything at all."

May we always rely on Christ, God, and the Holy Spirit as well! At this juncture, I would ask that each of you finish reading this book without pause. Give extra ears to the forthcoming scriptures, as we expand our look at my Eternal Victory Ranking list.

Keys to Heaven and Eternal Life Are Within Our Grasp!

1.	John 14:15	If you really love me, keep My Commandments.
2.	Eph. 4:1-6	One Lord - One Faith - One Baptism
3.	2nd Cor. 13:11	Be with the same agreeable mind, in Peace.
4.	1st Cor. 1:10-11	Let there be no divisions; be united in opinion.
5.	Rom. 16:16-18	Be on your guard, let no one mislead you
6.	Rom. 15:5-6	Encouragement in mutual harmony and full...
7.	Rom. 14:19	God grant us perfect harmony, united hearts.
8.	John 17:20-21, 26	Pursue Jesus in word and teaching, "rely on Me."
9.	Acts 18:8	Savior and Lord, many believed, and were saved.
10.	1st Cor. 7:19	Circumcision? No! Commandments of Christ? Yes!

How would you use the preceding? You might find a better way than I did and are free to use anything that might sound promising on this list, and certainly somewhere in the Good Book. Just imagine that if some of our rambunctious folks suddenly took the view of **"God will take care of us and this means that all is well. It's not necessary to focus on obeying the Commandments!"** This sounds a little far-fetched, but I and others on occasion throughout the years, perhaps when the minister was out of town that week, have heard questionable preaching come from the mouths of visiting ministers. Even hometown ministers can and do say things that sometimes lead to chaos. I'm not necessarily saying this about my community, but for sure in communities across the globe. I won't be reviewing specific statements in question!

Let's assume that we did hear this semi off-base comment in rapid fashion someplace. We would hope that it was a fast-passing comment that we misinterpreted. If we didn't misinterpret it, it certainly needs to be brought to the attention of whoever made the comment, right? What would you say to him? Right off, I would say, "Sir, I just want you to know that I did not hear what I thought I heard in your sermon today! Did you happen to say that we as Christians today do not have to obey the Commandments of God?" Obviously, this person would deny it, so the only thing we could do would be to smile and utter, "Wow, I knew we misunderstood you!"

If we lend our ten points to only **"Words that may Help Others and Ourselves,"** placing these words in as many one sentence statements we can think of in Bible language will result in a **worksheet of:**

Loving and Caring

Examples of Christian Love and Caring:

1.	**John 14:15**	**"Do you really love Me? Keep My Commandments!"**
2.	**Eph. 4:1-6**	**"Lead a worthy life of good behavior, humility, unselfishness, gentleness. Love one another, keep harmony and oneness produced by the Spirit. One Body, one Spirit, one hope, one Lord, one faith, one baptism, one God-Father of us all."**
3.	**2ⁿᵈ Cor. 13:11**	**"Rejoice, perfected, completed, what you ought to be; be encouraged, comforted; same mind one with another; live in peace, God of Love, Author and Promoter of peace will be with you."**
4.	**1ˢᵗ Cor. 1:10-11**	**"Agreement in what you say, no dissensions or factions or divisions among you, be perfectly united in your common understanding and in your opinions and judgments. Chole's**

		household--contentions and wrangling and factions among you."
5.	Rom. 16:16-18	"Brethren, be on guard concerning those who create dissensions and difficulties and cause divisions, in opposition to the doctrine (the teaching) which you have been taught. [I warn you to turn aside from them, to] avoid them."
6.	Rom. 15:5-6	"May God, Who... encouragement in such mutual harmony and full sympathy with one another in accord with Christ Jesus, That together you may [unanimously] with united hearts and one voice, praise and glorify the God and Father of our Lord Jesus Christ."
7.	Rom. 14:19	"Aim for and eagerly pursue what makes for harmony and for mutual upbuilding (edification and development) of one another."
8.	John 17:20-21, 26	"Neither for these alone do I pray...but also for all of those who will ever come to believe in (trust in, cling to, rely on) Me through their word and teaching, That they all may be one, [just] as You, Father, are in Me and I in You, that they also may be one in Us, so that the world may believe and be convinced that You have sent Me."
9.	Acts 18:8	"But Crispus, the leader of..believed [that Jesus is the Messiah and acknowledged Him with joyful trust as Savior and Lord], together with his entire household; and many of the Corinthians who listened to Paul also believed and were baptized."
10.	1st Cor. 7:19	Circumcision? No! - Commandments of Christ? Yes!

Looking At Our Mission

In a few words, our mission has been finding material that God, Christ, and the Holy Spirit generated to show the world what kind of people they expect to become citizens for eternity. This seems to me to be a great idea! From Their Words, we have developed what we consider to be among the best of selections for taking positive action in terms of assisting others to be completely Christian throughout.

111

In helping Congregations of Christ and other Christian-based institutions such as the example provided earlier in this chapter, I demonstrated what has to or what should be done with regard to broadening the scope of identification for those seeking truth about instrumental music vs. non instrumental music in worshiping God and His Son Jesus Christ.

I now seek the end of this true adventure about our training received in deciphering real questions and making use of that time with biblical studies and truly felt pain of being correct or incorrect about some of the comments made.

As you review the material on pages 109-111, you have at your disposal the meaning of scripture in various quantities that you can use as you see fit to find a solution to just about anything you might be researching. For example, #4 on page 109. We see that **1ˢᵗ Cor. 1:10-11** says, **"Let there be no divisions; be united,"** You probably have a good idea for what you just read. Let's pursue this on page 110, giving you more information than before for the same scripture! **1ˢᵗ Cor. 1:10-11** says, **"Agreement in what you say; no dissensions or factions or divisions among you; be perfectly united in your common understanding and in your opinion and judgments. Chole's household-- contentions and wrangling and factions among you."**

I cite another scripture, dividing it into two parts for more information! When you begin to work with additional scripture, always spend a bit more time in the exact, almost same location that you are currently studying. You will be surprised at the additional information received in your follow-up. It seems appropriate to read **2ⁿᵈ Cor. 13:11** on page 109, then skipping to page 110 for the remainder. It first reads, **"Be with the same agreeable mind, in Peace."** This is a great learning tool in my opinion! Compare this with the remainder of the verse, **"Rejoice, be perfected, completed, what you ought to be; be encouraged, comforted, of the same mind, one with another; live in peace, God of Love will be with you."**

So why change? What got in the way of merging two **congregations** into one? Let me show you and make a few comments. We recall that Minister (A)'s **congregation** has been using instrumental music in all their worship services for many years. At the same time, Minister (B)'s **congregation** only used their voices for worshiping in song. Ministers (A) and (B) were both very emotional and could hardly present their arguments without getting inwardly upset!

What is the problem? No Replies? Jesus knew, didn't He? They are battling one another simply because neither **congregation** could persuade the other. It's just that simple! Is this a human problem or a God problem? Know-it-all attitudes will bear few results. I give you my reasoning for saying what I just typed.

Look no further than Number #4 again: **1ˢᵗ Cor. 1:10-11 "...that all of you be in perfect harmony and full agreement in what you say, and that there be no dissensions or factions or divisions among you, but that you be perfectly united in your common understanding and in your opinions and judgments. v11 For it has been made clear to me, my brethren, by those of Chloe's household that there are contentions and wrangling and factions among you."**

This is a big Thought Statement! I believe that one great key to our Home in Eternity is to render obedience to God, Christ, and the Holy Spirit, then learn even more about what we have or have not obeyed. In so doing, we will be able to offer to others some of the material content about our insights from heaven, beginning with **John 15:15-16 (Jesus Speaking) "I do not call you servants (slaves) any longer, for the servant does not know what his Master is doing (working out). But I have called you My friends, because I have made known to you everything that I have heard from My Father. [I have revealed to you everything that I have learned from Him.] v16 You have not chosen Me, but I have chosen you and I have appointed you [I have planted you], that you might go and bear fruit and keep on bearing, and that your fruit may be lasting [that it remain, abide], so that whatever you ask the Father in My name [as presenting in all that I AM] He may give it to you."**

Dr. Stanley Morris - Greek and Hebrew Scholar!

The following material was found in The Christian Chronicle, February 2015. These Greek words of knowledgeable substance and Hebrew Scholarship in 1981, may have produced a completed translation of the New Testament, the Simple English Bible. Dr. Stanley Morris was at the forefront of a new Bible called the IEB (International English Bible). His work was introduced to the public. A few quotes of his work on page 21 of this Christian Chronicle publication are sufficient to introduce this scholar and his work to each of you. I quote Dr. Morris:

"We consistently use 'immerse' instead of 'baptize' and 'baptism' because of the original meaning of the Greek words, baptizo and baptisma." Dr. Morris then mentioned that William Tyndale, the Father of the English Bible, translated it as 'immersion.' He further stated that, "King James Version revisers changed it in A.D.

1611." He also said, "You will not find the English word 'Church' in the text of the IEB because that is a traditional rendering of the Greek word ekklesia."

The original Greek word always meant God's People, **NOT** an institution, a **church**, or a denomination. Those did not exist in the first century. Therefore, the word **church**, though familiar, is not an accurate translation. King James 1st deliberately chose the word **church** to replace the words as set forth by William Tyndale in the Holy Bible. You see, the word **church** was not an acceptable word; rather it went back to around 675 B.C.

The acceptable word for **church** is Ekklesia, the Greek word that Tyndale used when he completed the first correct English Bible. Ekklesia was to be translated to only one of two words, **Congregacion** and/or **Assembly**. No other words were acceptable until the great King James 1st in his own eyes, thought he had every right to direct others to make it his account, not Jesus the Christ. How terrible! Jesus did not want a **church**. He wanted a **Congregation** and/or **Assembly** of Christians, one that would agree with the structure and energy of the word, Ekklesia.

What Is Left To Be Said?

As we begin to try our best to put Wisdom in its proper place, we must use a system of critical thinking of times gone by and current thoughts that will give you what I believe to be, an absolute necessity in analyzing different situations. We have discussed much scripture and that is the quality part of Christianity. It goes without saying that the base of critical thinking in this book is the strong and direct placement of Scriptures from God, Jesus Christ, and the Holy Spirit. Every effort has been made to use the correct scripture that would let you know what now needs to be done. Once the scripture is designated, it then becomes the writer's choice of what to begin as a last step of the book or any other such activity.

As of now, I am charged with selecting a choice of action, as I am forced to come forth with the actions most appropriate to the concept that we must attend to in order to finish the task. The Task that now needs to be addressed is …. **Do not compromise your Biblical Knowledge simply to satisfy your newfound Christians-to-be (at least in principle) who wish to be immersed so they can quickly fit in with other Christians who are being added to your congregation! Why?**

Answering The Why

Realize for a moment that many **congregations** are rushing to find new Christians to place on a membership roll. In many respects this is great! However, keep in mind that there is much more to becoming a Christian than quickly saying "Immerse me." We need to remind ourselves that there is a belief that many Christian **congregations** fail to discuss the following kind of scriptures with Christians-to-be. It may be the umpteenth time we've looked at this, but I stress that excerpts from **1ˢᵗ Cor. 1:10-11** is scripture that soon-to-be Christians need to know. **"Agreement in what you say; no dissensions or factions or divisions among you, be perfectly united in your common understanding and in your opinions and judgments. Chloe's household---contentions and wrangling and factions believed to be among you."** One who wants to be a Christian needs to know a few things before he or she makes a final decision about immersion.

Interestingly, the following was from the 1st Century. This **congregation** was in fact being accomplished for Jesus by the Apostle Paul in a letter he had sent to the **congregation**, believed to have been somewhere around A.D. 52-55. This was part of the beginning of the establishment of Congregations of Christ. Be assured that workers for Christ were present at this location. Let's read from a completed translation by Tyndale, for Jesus, from **1ˢᵗ Cor. 16:19 "The congregacions of Asis salute you. Aquilla and Priscilla salute you mouche in the Lorde and so doeth the congregacion that is in their housse."**

Yes, a long time ago, Jesus and others took much time in establishing Christians, **NOT** Churches. What were they called? "ἐκκλησία" (**Congregacions** and/or **Assemblies**). They met in their houses for Bible Study or listened to Words of Truth. What would you say to an immersed believer? "You should go to **church**!" Or would you say, "You are the (ἐκκλησία)! That is, you are a member of the **Congregation** and/or **Assembly** of Christ, not a **church**! And as such, you are called a Christian." Let no one ever believe otherwise!

William Tyndale in his own way knew that Christ had told someone, perhaps Paul, to place in the original document which was the Old and New Testament, the fact that **"As Christians, the word church does not exist."** However, ἐκκλησία does exist and ἐκκλησία should be known only as a **Congregation** and/or **Assembly** of Christ.

I close this chapter by reading words spoken by Jesus in the **Book of John - Chapter 15.** May these words seep deeply into your heart!

v1 Jesus says, "I am the True Vine, and My Father is the Vinedresser.

v7 If you live in Me [abide vitally united to Me] and My words remain in you and continue to live in your hearts, ask whatever you will, and it shall be done for you.

v10 If you keep my commandments [if you continue to obey My instructions], you will abide in My love and live on in it, just as I have obeyed My Father's commandments and live on in His love.

v12 This is My commandment: that you love one another [just] as I have loved you.

v17 This is what I command you: that you love one another.

v18 If the world hates you, know that it hated Me before it hated you.

v23 Whoever hates Me also hates My Father."

Chapter Eleven

Is It The Words of Christ? Our Eternity Is Determined By Our Lives?

Words for Elders, Preachers and Members of The ἐκκλησία! Yes, this in many respects might be a time to look around and invest in words of years gone by and ask God to forgive us for failure to recognize what we have or have not done regarding the word ἐκκλησία. Very few of us have done much in our thinking, but wait! We try to draw closer to God, Christ, and the Holy Spirit to receive everything! Many of us have tried so hard to get somebody to do something and are beginning to wonder if there is anything that can be done! But there is someone there to help us. God, Christ, and the Holy Spirit!

It was about five years ago, right before I finished teaching a Bible class one Sunday morning, that I suggested it would be great if we could get others to meet with us and tackle this very question about the word **church**. No sooner was I finished with my lesson in the auditorium and using material from my first book, when an out of state visitor approached me and began to tell me that I've got to start believing that the **church** exists. What? I told him, "Well, I did use a big word like ἐκκλησία (ekklesia)," but he didn't know one thing about what it meant, nor was he willing to do anything but preach to me about the **church building** in which we were worshiping. His last words to me were something like, "Never lose word or sight of the **church**," with emphasis!

Again, take notice of who's being spoken to here. Elders, Preachers and Members of the ἐκκλησία. So far, my representative from the members category is none other than me and a good friend of mine! We continue to look around, not necessarily for the eldership, but for someone to get interested in the Ekklesia. What about the ministers? Yes, however, I find that most of the ministers I know are members of the Congregations of Christ, but really believe they are members of the Churches of Christ. Most do not know about the Congregations of Christ and they do not wish to learn about them! There has to be a solution to this problem. Well, let's talk about elders! Most elders that I know spend a great deal of time with ministers in determining the strategy for their **Congregations** and/or **Assemblies**. Don't get me wrong! Elders have a biblical function and most have a reason when they go to the minister to find out what might be done. When I share with them the word that I focus on in this book, there becomes a feeling that we must never change the word **church** to **Congregation** and/or **Assembly**. **Not Good!**

I'd like to talk more about preachers and elders and ask the question, "Why do you think they are so hesitant in taking action to change 'Churches of Christ' to 'Congregations of Christ' and expand their roles in trying to retain First Century Christianity, as spoken by many and certainly by Christ Jesus?" It seems like the answer is to keep using present-day words, as to not potentially upset people, allowing them to remain in their safe space while holding them back from the truth, as apparently dictated by Jesus Christ.

In Chapter Ten, you had the opportunity to see how it would have been written in early times. You also had the opportunity to look at typed scripture used by William Tyndale in the publication of the Old and New Testament in A.D. 1525-26. And by this time, even in A.D. 1611, you most certainly would have been able to read the New Testament printed by William Tyndale and reprinted as a new bible called King James Bible--Authorized Version.

Obviously, it's my intention to assist you in trying to show that King James 1st and his followers did a very foolish thing by rejecting what was inserted by Tyndale in translating the New Testament just as Jesus' spokesperson had translated it and as had been requested. That is, leave Ekklesia alone so that the manuscript, when **Congregation** and/or **Assembly** words were needed, would correctly address what Jesus had said, "Ekklesia." William Tyndale had written in A.D. 1525-26 what Jesus and His Father wanted. His original charge for English speakers was to develop a phrase of mighty words or sayings in a modified Koine Greek form, i.e., "I will build my ekklesia." So let's review.

He was successful, Thanks be to God! The word Ekklesia would only translate to **Assembly** and/or **Congregacion**. The word that was used by King James' translators was the word Kuriakon, used approximately 675 years before Christ was born in the Jerusalem area. There was underhandedness in doing it this way for the following reason. Ekklesia (ἐκκλησία) was not compatible with the word Kuriakon. The translators for King James would have understood not to use that which had changed from language to language.

By Faith we Believe. By Holiness we show Understanding. By Love we demonstrate Kindness. This Is Christian Living! Faith, Understanding and Kindness quickly define us as members of a Congregation of Christ. The essential ingredient is a product of the three words Belief–Holiness- Kindness. These three words equal a product known as a Follower of Jesus.

It shows that we are completing the beginning and ending of what Jesus told us to do in His scriptures, resulting in us to live as He told us to live in those same New Testament scriptures! We are indeed a blessed People! We can easily equate the meaning of the scriptures that were used in my Eternal Victory Ranking list on page

89 with the words that Jesus often used above. A look back will show this to be true.

Those men and women who have watched a touch of Wisdom grow into a mountain of Knowledge have experienced and are generally blessed with a comprehensive way of life. This calls upon parents and the growing young man or lady to spend more time on results of applied wisdom, the kind of life that becomes focused upon concerns we have about destinations. It takes a very close family to make the outcome successful.

Thus far, we have tried to set in motion preceding activities that bring precedence to our thoughts and actions, leading to success. You will recall earlier that emphasis was placed on the kind of men and women that rise to the occasion of mastery of whatever it is that has been planned. The planning does not happen overnight!

We remember the kind of useful words or actions that are used to bring us what we're truly seeking in ourselves or others. Jesus used words to get our attention as we grow to satisfy ourselves, but most importantly, satisfy what our Lord wants. If we can satisfy our Lord Jesus, we will be satisfied with what we did to satisfy Him! I'll use a very short scripture to justify this. Jesus said in **John 14:15, "If you love Me keep My Commandments!"** Can it be any more straightforward than this? Love Him, Keep His Commandments and show Him that as we grow to satisfy ourselves, we also recognize the joy of satisfying what our Lord wants.

We've spent a great deal of time looking at 1st Cor. 1:10-11, scripture dealing with the attitudes of people. The Apostle Paul is sharing words of Life with those who are becoming preachers, elders and just solid citizens! There were several people as it seems, preparing to go out and convert others to become adept in the Word of God and the cause of Christ. That is, preparing them for present and Everlasting Life, so they can teach others what they have been taught. Paul's intent was to teach all how to be kind, loving and caring, immersing them in the name of Jesus our Lord. Chloe's household was used as a place to keep Christians or would-be Christians while they were away from their homes and in all likelihood, many probably didn't have homes of their own.

So what is lacking as this journey continues? Let's play a role for Christ Jesus. We'll pretend to be His helpers! Hopefully, we've already begun. We have been reminded that each Congregation of Christ stands on its own as a part of God's One Body of Believers. We have learned that a **Congregation** and/or an **Assembly** is preferable in worshiping God than a so-called formal **church**, laden with wealth for so many unnecessary things.

Do These Questions Make You Uneasy?

1.   Does the fact that Jesus in His own way gave William Tyndale the initial work of translating and printing an Old and New Testament in Greek words, bother you? Indeed, Tyndale was able to translate and bring to press both Old and New Testaments in English, prior to his death when he was ridiculously convicted of heresy, strangled and burned at the stake.

2.   Would it bother you in trying to find Christians who have learned to think like God, Jesus, and the Holy Spirit, to try to get the world straightened out in recognizing that scripture from one language doesn't always fit the way we think it should? How do you think Jesus feels about doing His best to get what He wanted from William Tyndale, as opposed to what he really got, but didn't want, that being the wrong Greek word (Kuriakon)? I strongly believe that Jesus doesn't want people to engage in the word **church**. That word had already been ruined for the souls of many. How? The words **Congregation** and/or **Assembly** are full of what Jesus really wanted prior to King James' theft.

I say with all my being that I believe that Jesus really wants to have the word **church** removed from any text. He never wanted Tyndale to use it and he didn't. He used the word Ekklesia, (ἐκκλησία). We had the significant and truthful word for **Congregation** and/or **Assembly**! Jesus had what He wanted and had asked for!

The real puzzle of my life is wondering why members of the ἐκκλησία didn't help change the course of direction when King James 1ˢᵗ made the move to change **congregation** to **church**. I am beginning to believe that only Jesus, God and the Holy Spirit knew of the imminent change and that the use of the word **church** would be purposely continued by those who disagreed with William Tyndale's remarkable work at the direction of Jesus Christ!

Do you suppose we Christians could have helped turn this around when this took place in 1611? Why do you say Yes? Why do you say No? Would you have been afraid of the Fix had you been there? King James 1ˢᵗ had at his disposal an army of many! This undoubtedly was a frightful time to the common people living within the region. I must only believe that this was in the hands of Jesus, who took care of it or will take care of it come the day of Judgment! I say all this comparatively because I know of only a handful of preachers who in any way have publicly stood up and made statements for rectification. It would be very difficult to name anyone except Christ and/or God. At the same time, several excellent authors have written outstanding material on the subject, some of which I've placed in this book! The substance is good and it's honest. In my humble opinion, Christians are needed in much bigger numbers to support those willing to take up the cause of exposing the dreadful results of the hijacking of two words that belong to Christ; **Congregation** and/or **Assembly**, not **church**. Perhaps the only power we have to deal with this dilemma is Kindness!

And how is it that we can execute this kind of Power? Jesus taught us that kindness is Power, used correctly. The power to change our attitudes! The power to change attitudes of others if done correctly. What power did Jesus have when He was wronged, time and time again? The answer! The Power of Love and Kindness. We have listed the sources of this many times in this book. It deals with biblical language enumerated by our Lord!

My Own Study That I Feel Obligated To Share

I pray that my comments in the next couple of pages will contain Words of Wisdom from the Word of God, to the Touch of Christ, and the Comfort of the Holy Spirit. You have absorbed scripture in this book and can make your words be heard in almost any action needed to benefit the listener. I believe Words of Wisdom have in one place or another been used as positive models to close this chapter.

The measurement of a man or woman in parenting or spiritual maturity is somewhat dependent upon the instruction and care each has or has not received early on in their life. Most parents that I know and know well, at times have not been the ideal symbols for raising mature and good-natured children. The reason? Too little attention from each working parent and too much attention from friends and/or siblings. Hopefully I am not being overly critical nor polite, because this is a mark of early wisdom concerning the growth of children. If parents hold back too much attention from one child, siblings may also receive too little attention and that often takes the child out of his/her proper attention span and out of what may be considered ample conditional coverage! Yet most parents who admit to this kind of rearing are ready, capable and excellent in what they have learned and/or quickly learning over a span of time.

Who Is In Charge At Home In Terms Of Religious Activities?

In most Congregations of Christ, we see husbands and wives at the headship of the family of worshipers; to stand, be accounted and worship as our God directs. Obviously, this includes men who are chosen as elders and deacons in activities related to God, Christ and the Holy Spirit. It includes women, not as elders, but as teachers and vital participants in worshiping with a **congregation** of Christian people along with their children. Togetherness is a beautiful thing in a service of Christians worshiping as a family. It is even more beautiful when men assume the role of leading their family as a wholesome collection of God's Children, worshiping Jesus Christ, thanking God Almighty for His Creation and direction, and the Holy Spirit for guidance that is given to mankind.

Needless to say, if women decide to meet as a group of Christian Women, may it be so without interference from man. Simply touch base with a minister or an elder and get material from them that may be helpful in making your bible studies powerful in the sight of God!

When your **congregation** decides to act as two, elders must take the initiative, be as orderly as possible and give directives as needed. Regardless of the number of elders in your **congregation**, all of them must remind each other that they report to Jesus the Savior, Almighty God, and the Holy Spirit. Obviously, all should report in their own way! Prayer serves to calm and get most people collected to serve as they should! If the minister's actions appear to be divisive, it may be the head elder that needs to talk with the other elders, subsequently demanding that the preacher stop pitting members against each other. You might also be surprised at the number of times that ministers and other leaders within the **congregation** may ask for your help!

Families committed to God, Jesus, and the Holy Spirit, cherish the genuine assistance from other well-trained and experience-filled families who have already gone through times that were theirs to endure. The help provided might be of great service to those that tend to be a bit unruly and/or a bit noisy in their movement. How else can I say this? They will most likely accept your wisdom and knowledge of appropriate behavior. Keep in mind that most people and their families are willing and able to do their parts in maintaining a real place to worship in Spirit and Truth!

Chapter Twelve

The Great Power Of Love And Kindness

The Truth is when one is reading the Word of God, he or she will come across many words that are inspired by Jesus Christ. One such instance of this is **2ⁿᵈ Cor. 13:11 "Be strengthened...be encouraged and consoled and comforted, be of the same [agreeable] mind one with another, live in peace, and [then] the God of Love [who is the source of affection, goodwill, love, and benevolence toward men] and the Author and Promoter of peace will be with you."** We see another helpmate to victory through Love in **John 14:15 "If you [really] love Me, you will keep (obey) my commands."** Yes, there is a whole verse of thought in this one scripture on gaining Hope and Calmness to attain Christ's Blessing! Try the following: **John 15:10 "If you keep my commandments [If you continue to obey My instructions], you will abide in My love and live on in it, just as I have obeyed My Father's commandments and live on in His love."** How can we ask for anything better than this? Perhaps **John 15:17 "This is what I command you: that you love one another."**

Our Christlike Mediator Is Once Again Called Upon

A situation arises whereby your younger and very good singers have approached an elder whom you know as a friend, asking that the **congregation** start a new music group, one that would work to enthusiastically better the singing with newer songs of praise, veering away from a sole song leader and increasing participation. The potential problem? The elder they've approached likes the idea, but also suggests musical instruments to lead the new group. On the other hand, another older elder in the **congregation** has declared that things simply function better when you have a Congregation of Christians who sing in a manner that's perceived by many to be biblically correct, that being A Capella.

For an answer that might work, we bring Dr. Roger Harrell back into the picture, once again taking on the role of a Christlike mediator. He says at the first meeting pertaining to the possible new music group, "My good friends, young and old. Don't think for a minute that all of us older folks are in line to become the next resident in a nursing home. We may move and think slower than we used to, but our ability of discernment is as prevalent as it ever was. We are truly a good people that want what's best for all in the eyes of God (Everyone smiles). I have known many of you for more than 40 or 50 years. Today's discussion should center around what your **congregation** needs, not wants. Did God authorize us to use instrumental music? I must admit that I have searched for an answer for the last 65 years and as of yet, I haven't found one. We can search and search until we die. God will help us sing with instruments if He really meant for us to do so. With regard to your mainly younger members who would really like to see a group of A Capella singers lead your **congregation** in songs of praise instead of a sole song leader; I couldn't agree more and I say this as a former song leader myself for many years. As for the group to be accompanied by instruments, let's table the issue for 50 days. Spend time in prayer and also with one another. I would encourage the young to visit with the old and for the old to reach out to the young. I would also urge your **congregation** to do its best in eliminating any cliques amongst you, young or old, as you are One Body of Believers worshiping together. Acting as you are indeed One Body will definitely help you in your decision-making abilities. Our next and maybe last meeting will be in about 50 days."

Fifty Day Wait Is Over - Same Opinion Provided As Earlier

The fifty day wait is over and Dr. Harrell is present once again. He has been given a lot of information by leaders and members of the **congregation**. He briefly states, "Thank you and thanks to all who have prayerfully considered what's at hand. Based upon all the Biblical data that I have seen and that you have shared with me, I must disappointingly state for some that my recommendation is to maintain status quo at this **congregation** concerning musical instruments until an overwhelming majority leans one way or the other."

Now I want to bring a true story to you firsthand and tell you what has taken place in a similar situation at the **congregation** in which my family and I worship. It is a **congregation** with an estimated 200 to 300 members depending on the time of year since the mountain village is much more populated with tourists in the summer, many of them staying for several months. It is a great **congregation** with an excellent preacher, wonderful youth minister and great elders.

The elders and ministers contemplated bringing instrumental music into the **congregation** every other Wednesday evening. A majority of them made the choice to do so, not realizing at the time that there were many members worshiping there that would not be pleased at all. The date was set for a decision and on that particular Sunday, it was announced that instrumental music would make its appearance every other Wednesday. About 25 of us approached the elders to see if it would be possible that this decision might be rescinded. A time was set for discussion and most of the elders were present along with those who were against this move. Dissenters presented very good reasons in my opinion. The long and the short was, within a week it was announced that the elders would rescind its decision of instrumental music for an unknown period of time. I believe the decision was a good one for the **congregation** and the 18% or so that would have left (about the usual percentage), who were now feeling upbeat and thankful to the Trinity. Ultimately, instruments did make their way into services every other Wednesday and the 18% or so did leave and formed a new **congregation**. The good thing about the partial split was that there didn't appear to be any hard feelings or animosity between those who left and those who stayed, many of them still great friends today.

Manners And Reasons Make A Huge Difference

The elders and ministers who are in charge of congregational change, planning or assistance in forthcoming programs, must stand and be ready to serve. Sometimes with a Yes and often with a No. Let me say this a different way! Let's plan things in a manner that will yield the most fruit, praying that God, Christ and the Holy Spirit will help us achieve victory in whatever project or program we might be developing.

The biggest problem I see in years ahead, centuries to come or whatever time is left prior to Judgment Day, is that of local **congregations** across the world trying their best with appropriate or inappropriate leadership, to ready their **congregations** so as to touch all the bases of what I would like to suggest. Simply stated, how do we learn from now until the day of Judgment? I want to share something that I truly thought would work when I began to develop this material. I did something with my writing that I've never really done before. The approach that I generally use is to set forward the essence of the book early on and then keep a useful theme that leads to the accomplishment of the main goal, and or goals!

Here's a simple plan for whatever it is that you wish to do to in helping to place Christian congregations in action with the idea of solving large or small problems and with very little friction! Recall a few of the ideas that we earlier brought to light concerning Christian congregations. You were asked to read the words as they appeared in New Testament times as written by William Tyndale. It was one of the first real versions of Koine Greek that was translated into Old (Ole) English. You began to see what the Language of Christ was. The Congregation of Christ stands on its own as a part of **God's Congregation**. You found 10 critical points of scripture on pages 109-111. As you review these spiritual directives again, you will have at your disposal the means to find a solution to just about anything you're confronted with.

The Finality

When facing some kind of Congregational showdown, I consider the final pursuit of action to be one involving a tiptoe to the answer, especially if you're an elder or minister! Here's the question and it's time for us to solve the problem! What is the problem? You have a group of people in your **congregation** that are faithful Christians to the core. They think instrumental music would be a Godsend to your program of worship. What would you do? This is a question that's very much a reality for the Body of Christ in God's World today! I believe the following steps hold real value as you work toward a beneficial solution.

STEP ONE: As soon as you find out exactly what the people have requested in order to have a more viable **congregation**, list all of their reasons. I believe you as an elder, deacon or minister need to take one first step. That is to survey the entire **congregation** with a short paper questionnaire. It can be as simple as Yes or No! Find out how many Christians in your **congregation** want to bring instrumental music to center and find out how many want to keep it as it has been for whatever number of years! You won't really know unless you take this first step.

Believe it or not, most **congregations** don't ever take the first step. Why? They believe it can be solved with a touch of tone, for they are the elders and ministers! I know, as I have been one as well! But let's assume now that the percentage of For and Against was around 50-50! Wouldn't it bother you to not find out one way or another? Can you think of another way to ascertain the information that you want and badly need?

Two groups are wanting different outcomes. One group wants to sing with instruments during worship and the other without. Anything that the elders and ministers say may be wrong in the eyes of each group. How do you respond to this? You must tell them the truth. The elders and ministers would like to have another vote, at which time they will see if the percentage has changed. They are asking for members of each group to meet several times in the next 50 days before another poll is taken. Until then, both groups continue to be servants of God and do their very best to draw closer together and closer to God.

STEP TWO: Let the **congregation** know what the vote was as soon as possible and ask the minister to preach a sermon on growth and understanding in a neutral tone at your next Lord's Day Service. Have them give the pros and cons of singing with instrumental music versus what may be perceived by many to be the scriptural thing to do.

STEP THREE: Several meetings have now taken place in the preceding 50 days. Time to call a special Sunday night meeting for all members. Depending on the passion exhibited by both groups, you might be lucky if a handful show up or you might have a full house. After a few minutes of listening to praise by the minister along with several songs being sung by those present, the minister begins to look at the results of the most recent vote as well as a few notes from the elders. All of the data is ready to be presented. It's presented by the minister and indicates a change of heart, as 37% of the ballots are marked Yes for instrumental music with the percentage against having grown to 63%. It's important to realize that approximately 18% of non-instrumental worshiping Christians will leave for other **congregations** of Christians in their area when a hasty decision is made by elders and ministers with regard to the introduction of instrumental music.

STEP FOUR: With the push for instrumental music having lost ground in the last vote, you can imagine there are happy and less than happy folks. Recall that the minister spoke to the groups several times and instead of getting on his high horse and condemning the instrumental group for even thinking about wanting the **congregation** to endure a pretty drastic change, he used great judgment and spoke about things in a biblical tone that was understood by all.

STEP FIVE: When biblical words are spoken, positive things happen! Throughout this book, I have attempted to use many of the same scriptures that should be viewed as winners in the eyes of us all. You've read the following scripture several times by now, words for calming those who may be overly eager in what they desire, but given time they will better understand with the help of Jesus. Success will follow in comprehending the full concept of what the word of Jesus can do. **1ˢᵗ Cor. 1:10 "But I urge and entreat you brethren, by the name of our Lord Jesus Christ, that all of you be in perfect harmony and full agreement in what you say, and that there be no dissensions or factions or divisions among you."** What? All in Perfect Harmony and Full Agreement, and No Dissensions or Factions or Divisions? **THIS is Our Charge** in the name of Jesus the Messiah! Who among us would ever deny the power of God, Christ, or the Holy Spirit?

An important point! If you are a minister or an elder, no one has a greater opportunity than you in keeping your flock together if you'll follow all of the steps.

I would always exclude the word **church**. I believe that Jesus put into place two words that could be used to tell the world what we are all about. Instead of the word **church** being used, Tyndale correctly brought ekklesia to us in English from ἐκκλησία in Koine Greek, translating as **Congregation** and/or **Assembly**, not **church**.

STEP SIX: Let's use words and ideas that should be in the vocabulary of each Christian. These are words that seem to turn quickly to the side of Honesty, Glory and Heaven. Consider **by Faith we can Believe, by Holiness we can develop understanding and by Love we will display it!** In the Christian vocabulary, Kindness is Power! The Power of Love and Kindness leads us to Manners and Reason and this makes all the difference in the world when searching for solutions. A Touch of Wisdom leads to answers! Sometimes the only Power we have to deal with a dilemma is Kindness! Jesus taught us that Kindness is Power! The Power to change our attitudes! The Power to change attitudes of others! Jesus displayed the power of love and kindness whenever he was wronged by someone! Each Congregation of Christ stands on its own as a part of God's One Ekklesia- ἐκκλησία!

I've always thought that the latter pages of any religious book should contain content that will speak words of Wisdom from the Word of God to the Touch of Christ and the Comfort of the Holy Spirit! When one **congregation** decides to act as two, elders must take the initiative to be as orderly as possible and as directive as need be!

2nd Cor. 13:11 "Be strengthened...be encouraged and consoled and comforted; be of the same [agreeable] mind one with another; live in peace, and [then] the God of Love [who is the source of affection, goodwill, love, and benevolence toward men] and the Author and Promoter of peace will be with you!"

Something that might be paramount to you someday centers upon elders and ministers. The entire **congregation** should be given the opportunity of saying Yes or No to a short informational statement of intentions. If the elders of any **congregation** do not have some mention of what is taking place prior to it happening, there will be many more people in that **congregation** saying, "I wish I had known that this was going to take place." Immediately, this lack of communication has switched the "It's okay" to "I don't appreciate being left out!" And finally, **Rom. 14:19 "So let us then definitely aim for and eagerly pursue what makes for harmony and for mutual upbuilding (edification and development) for one another."**

STEP SEVEN: Here are some general suggestions that you can refer to at some point on down the road, based on my experiences in the Eldership at various **congregations**. This is the final step! Seven is a number that oftentimes represents Completeness. I assure you that I will continue to offer you God's promises, Christ's assurances and the Holy Spirit's indwelling in us.

Looking at **John 14:15-20** Jesus said, **"If you [really] love Me, you will keep (obey) My Commands. v16 And I will ask the Father, and He will give you another Comforter (Counselor, Helper, Intercessor, Advocate, Strengthener, and Standby) that He may remain with you forever----, v17 The Spirit of Truth, Whom the world cannot receive (welcome, take to its heart), because it does not see Him or know or recognize Him. But you know and recognize Him, for He lives with you [constantly] and will be in you. v18 I will not leave you as orphans [comfortless, desolate, bereaved, forlorn, helpless]; I will come back to you."** And now a wonderful closing couple of verses to this passage of scripture. **v19 "Just a little while now, and the world will not see Me anymore, but you will see Me; because I live, you will live also. v20 At that time [when that day comes] you will know [for yourselves] that I am in My father, and you are in Me, and I am in you."**

We've taken what seems like a long ride together up to this point. Thanks for being with me and although I may not know you, I hope to see you someday, either here on earth or in Heaven. Some words of advice for you and others. You may be worshiping with a great set of elders and a great person who preaches the Word of God. Never be afraid to offer advice to these leaders, for they are just like you and me. They need your help! Tell them on occasion how you feel! Strive to live by the truth found in the Word of God and by the truths that you are most likely reading about for the first time in this book. Share all of these truths with your friends and family, for I believe what you are reading may indeed give you a feeling of assuredness. Never be afraid of offering ways to improve to those with whom you work and/or those with whom you worship! If you face rejection of the truths you speak about, brush it off and continue on in your journey.

By the time you're finished with this book, I imagine you might have the scripture below memorized. I believe there's as much, if not more, Christian teaching in this one scripture than in any other that I can recall. May you richly be blessed and may your days be many! **1st Cor. 1:10 "But I urge and entreat you brethren, by the name of our Lord Jesus Christ, that all of you be in perfect harmony, and full agreement, in what you say, and that there be no dissensions, or factions or divisions among you, perfectly united in your common understanding, and in your opinions and judgments."**

Chapter Thirteen

Delivering Solid Congregational Guidance

What spirit have we been listening to? That which belongs to the world or the Holy Spirit Who is from God? We'll begin to find an answer in **1ˢᵗ Cor. 2:12-13 "Now we have not received the spirit [that belongs to] the world, but the [Holy] Spirit Who is from God, [given to us] that we might realize and comprehend and bless the gifts [of divine favor and blessing so freely and lavishly] bestowed on us by God. v13 And we are setting these truths forth in words not taught by human wisdom but taught by the [Holy] Spirit, combining and interpreting spiritual truths with spiritual language [to those who possess the Holy Spirit.]"** Yet this is not the final story regarding the Holy Spirit Who is from God.

Keep the passage above in mind while reading[14] **Matt. 22:31-46**. This deals with a simple issue that our elders and ministers could have examined in the previous chapter with regard to aspects of their final judgment. Critical to this judgment is the willingness to be firm, but never overbearing. Do not ever back yourself into a level of panic if trying to meet a deadline or you could end up making decisions and statements that you may regret. God will not be rushed, but we don't have His assurance that we will not be rushed. Why not be the one person on your team of congregational leaders that is looked up to with respect to timelines, thoughtfulness and superior planning.

Most preachers that I know are members of various **congregations**, yet they know little or nothing about the Ekklesia. Most elders that I know spend a great deal of time with their ministers in determining the strategy for their **Congregations** and/or **Assemblies**. Elders and deacons truly have biblical functions and you can find them in **Tit. 1:6-7, Acts 14:23, Tit. 1:5, Tit. 3:1-7, Tit. 5:17, Acts 20:29-31, Acts 20:28, Tit. 1:9** and **James 5:14**.

Whether you be a minister, elder or deacon, you must give loving guidance to members of your **congregation**. This is your responsibility! The Body of Christians you serve have great love for you and will do almost whatever you wish in serving our God. One of your tasks is to identify the limits, then know what is necessary to maintain the limits. This is no small task, but you will handle it with care I am sure!

---

[14] https://www.biblegateway.com/passage/?search=matthew+22%3A31-46&version=AMP

If I were asked this morning to name one thing above all others that would cause growth of Character and Maturity at our Congregations of Christ, I would say Unity. Unity means Oneness! It means no dissensions! To be unified is to be united in Thought, Purpose, Spirit, and Action. The Integrity, Honesty, and Sincerity of each individual must be beyond reproach in order for Harmony and Unity to exist. Unity is following the words of Christ for Peace and Harmony, with all ingredients incorporated in the words we have been reading!

However, there are many times that Jesus and His workers fill the air around us with caution. Remember what we looked at earlier when the Apostle Paul gave comfort and appealed to his brethren in **Rom. 16:17**? He said, **"I appeal to you, brethren, to be on your guard concerning those who create dissensions and difficulties and cause divisions, in opposition to the doctrine (the teaching) which you have been taught. [I warn you to turn aside from them, to] avoid them."**

Scripture-wise, we stand in excellent company. The difficult part of bringing oneness to a multipurpose **congregation** is the possibility that a clique of members might want to become the designated group to break ranks and try something new! Unfortunately, this leads to prejudices. It might work and it might not! Why take the chance as you lead the sheep to safety? This and other questions mandate legitimate answers. We cannot afford to do something that brings a flicker of hope for new life ---- and then Nothing!

Whoever you are and wherever you are, you can be a vital part of an excellent **congregation**. Do you know of a **congregation** trying to increase its membership by attracting people who will simply conform to anything they're told? And at what price? Think about it! I believe with all my heart that every **congregation** across the globe must take a stand with known biblical practices that we traditionally grew up with. Are we doing things in His **congregations** correctly? Incorrectly? I don't want to sound legalistic, but study the Bible! If you can find errors in the New Testament, make the necessary changes. If not, don't meddle with it! Think about it! Pray about it! Talk to God About it Regularly! Don't forget to talk Regularly with the God that will not turn from anyone if that person wishes to LEARN from HIM!

Chapter Fourteen

Tyndale Carefully Chose His Words – A Work Of God

Several people in Tyndale's time have without doubt told of his use of time, much of which is mentioned in this chapter. Tyndale was a strong, gifted man. Yes, this is correct! He continued as such in several notable cases. He deliberately chose to render words that had a long legacy in Catholicism, replacing them with new terms that Catholics found offensive. For example, he used **Congregation** instead of **church**, Elder instead of Priest, Repent instead of Do Penance and Love instead of Charity. Tyndale's English translation of these words were in many cases probably more familiar Vulgate, upon which much Christian theology had been based. These changes were offensive to Catholics and were heavily criticized by many, including Tyndale's countryman, Thomas More. Interestingly enough, the King James translators chose to retain the traditional terms, including **church**, Priest and Charity, but nowhere does one find the word Penance in the King James version. Penitent is defined in the dictionary as follows, although it requires a bit of straightening out. Penitent from Websters is read as, "one who is feeling or expressing sorrow for sin of wrong-doing and disposed to atonement and amendment; repentant; contrite." What is Penance? Again, from Webster's Encyclopedic Unabridged Dictionary of the English Language, Penance is defined as 1) a punishment undergone in token of penance or 2) a penitential disciple imposed by **church** authority, or 3) a sacrament, as in the Roman Catholic Church, consisting in a confession of sin, made with sorrow and with the intention of amendment, followed by forgiveness.

I believe that you and I have executed a quality bit of reading that truly gives support to our God, our Christ and our Holy Spirit. (Remember, it is often that Jesus Christ called upon The Holy Father). I also think that you have done a great job of attending to the many scriptures you have read and are digesting at this very moment, information that reflects your grasp of the Word of God, His Son and the Holy Spirit.

I use the words (1) **Final Caution** along with (2) **Blessed Farewell** to arrive at the special words of (3) **Patience/Courage** and (4) **Eternal Life**. Let's help everyone to be very cautious in this life, working with one another and more accepting of our courage to simply rely on the Words of God, Jesus and the Holy Spirit. Well, this is one teaching that I almost gave away. What was it?

Very Simply: Use Final Caution to assure Blessed Farewell! This to me involves two things in all that we may do to assure ourselves, family and friends of a Blessed Farewell and Eternal Life. The third item is a combination of Patience and Courage and the fourth item would be helping to ensure the presence of a forward look to Eternal Life through Righteousness, consisting of Love, Kindness and Happiness in our own lives lived here on earth while looking toward Heaven and Eternity. It may be stated a bit differently, but it remains the same. I have hinted many times that our actions from here to eternity should be filled with gratitude and goodwill to all who listen to and work with us to ready our souls!

Why?

I believe that many are holding one foot in the ring, hoping that it will stay there on its own accord!

Remember?

At the same time, let me assure you that I try to love all people equally and no time can really be the right time, unless there are a number of times the things that were on the right have suddenly turned to the left and they found another way they thought would work better. And it could! Perhaps. Onward !!

The words above will lead others to Higher Ground and we will follow if not already there. If you feel you are locked into this pattern, hold on to this direction unless you receive knowledge of something else that you truly must do to honor those who are beckoning to you to come to Me (what I believe Jesus would say)! I've heard voices from many pulpits giving directions to many folks. The directions are very good, but when spoken to worshipers, just how are they receiving the Truth from the mouths who are a bit off the beaten path at times?

A Real Concern

As Christians grow older, they seem to me to be ready to exchange what they believe they should do for God, Christ, and the Holy Spirit, as the timeline of Faith affects them. This of course affects almost everything that they have been doing versus what they should be doing. It could become a very volatile action and they should measure this with all of the wisdom they can muster from their growth toward God, Jesus and the Holy Spirit!

I do not mind sharing with you my last effort in assessing my last real concern to measure up to the Glory that we all shall anticipate from the Father, the Son, and The Holy Spirit. I hold sacred those things that I have learned up to my grasp of His Word to know without a doubt. First, I am convinced that as a part of a world body of Christ, we must indeed accept the fact that we still have differences and that we must hold to the truths that we believe strongly are acceptable to the Trinity and ourselves. I have already shared with you some of my feelings about the limited feelings of many of my friends.

My true feelings of things as they now stand are very much in tune with my spiritual leaders, yet I can tell you that not all agree with me. When I disagree with **congregation** leaders or even my own remote structure of families about some of the content in this book, I sense a feeling from some that they are let down because I was not completely in tune with what **congregation** leaders at my own house of worship were thinking. For me to say they are wrong and I am right sounds to me to be out of line. For me to say they are right and I am wrong would be false in my eyes because I have these strong feelings of Faith in the Trinity.

Chapter Fifteen

Live By A Page of Rights Until Experiences Cause Change!

This is a Page of Rights that I must live with until the Page of Rights that I own become a Page of Wrongs to cause me to adjust my Present Wrongs to Rights. My Page of Rights are as follows:

I accept the fact that The Trinity asked for Christians to become a part of the Worldwide Body within a structure designed to portray what a personified Christian may or may not do! This seems to me that it permits Christians to strive to ascertain the parts of the Body to seek a structure of each Congregation of Christ that stands on its own as a part of God's One Ekklesia- ἐκκλησία! It also says to the world that qualifications are being established.

All **congregations** who can or will soon be able, should immediately review the qualifications of Christian Citizenship. Have you as a Body of Christ taken time to tap into the possibilities of the Trinity assisting you in closely examining what kind of help has been given to Christians at your location? Has this received any attention from your ministers, deacons or elders? If not, why not? It should be very important to you!

And now I have a very good question to pose to you. Do you believe that your **congregation** and its members are getting the quality instruction that you feel they need? If your answer is yes, it is simply a great blessing. If there is a need, is there a way of providing it to them without creating so much friction that could very well destroy any great thinking?

I must tell you of my feelings of being close to the end of this book. In just a few words, I say to all readers, **Our Thanks be to God, Jesus and the Holy Spirit!** The totality of my feelings about the remaining pathway left for you and me is simple. **It will require vigor, alertness and conscientiousness!** It will not all be easy, nor will it be that difficult! However, it will require wisdom, steadfastness and vigor of heart. It, above all, will call on each of us to Love one another. The greatest force found for any worthwhile activity depends on us as His children. As you read this, you may be puzzled at times about the direction that I would take as I close out a story of this magnitude.

I believe we should seek a strong and Righteous God, Christ and the Holy Spirit to lead the way and where possible, use the WAY to tackle the issue of keeping our loved ones, ourselves and as many others as possible, invigorated with quality actions. I'll again share a very familiar verse that to me epitomizes an action of certainty. You've memorized it by now, right?

1st Cor. 1:10 "But I urge and entreat you brethren, by the name of our Lord Jesus Christ, that all of you be in perfect harmony and full agreement in what you say, and that there is no dissensions or factions or divisions among you, but that you be perfectly united in your common understanding and in your opinions and judgments." This last Driving, Powerful string of words is held up by you, me and other Christians from all parts of this World as guided by God Our Creator, Christ The Savior and The Holy Spirit!

You will recognize the following Christian words as fit for action! It would be hard to find another group of biblical words more beneficial for us than these beautiful words of wisdom. We start by looking at three questions concerning harmony and then continue. **2nd Cor. 6:15-18** says, **"What harmony can there be between Christ and Belial [the Devil]? Or what has a believer in common with an unbeliever? v16 What agreement [can there be between] a temple of God and idols? For we are the Temple of the living God, even as God said, I will dwell in and with and among them and will walk in and with and among them, and I will be their God, and they shall be My people."** How could anyone change the answer to these questions if God did not change a people that could or would understand Him? **v17 "So, come out from among [unbelievers], and separate (sever) yourselves from them, says the Lord, and touch not [any] unclean thing, then I will receive you kindly and treat you with favor, v18 And I will be a Father to you, and you shall be my sons and daughters, says the Lord Almighty."** And another meaningful scripture of action. **Eph. 4:3 "Be eager and strive earnestly to guard and keep the harmony and oneness of [and produced by] the Spirit in the binding power of peace."**

I believe that if I were you, I would take the time to read again, alone or with others, the first six chapters. By the time you will have read all of these chapters, you should have a good grasp of purpose and of the business of the Holy Spirit, the Blessed Savior Jesus, and The Father of us all, our Blessed Creator.

This chapter comes to a close with more powerful words of action found in **1st Peter 3:11-15 "Let him turn away from wickedness and shun it and let him do right. Let him search for peace (harmony, undisturbedness from fears, agitating passions, and moral conflicts) and seek it eagerly. [Do not merely desire peaceful** relations with God, with your fellowmen, and with yourself, but pursue, go after them!] v12 For the eyes of the Lord are upon the righteous (those who are upright and in right standing with God) and His ears are attentive to their prayer. But the face of the Lord is against those who practice evil [to oppose them, to frustrate, and defeat them]. v13 Now who is there to hurt you if you are zealous followers of that which is good? v14 But even in case you should suffer for the sake of righteousness, [you are] blessed, happy to be envied. Do not dread or be afraid of their threats, nor be disturbed [by their opposition]. v15 But in your hearts set Christ apart as holy [and acknowledge Him] as Lord. Always be ready to give a logical defense to anyone who asks you to account for the hope that is in you, but do it courteously and respectfully."

Chapter Sixteen

Bidding You Farewell

What a feeling! Am I too old and too biased to express my innermost satisfaction with the outcome of this journey? Please excuse me! I just cannot help it! I wanted so much to write a book for solid and worthwhile outcomes and I feel pleased to have you as my guest of honor and to be able to provide a path for a better understanding. Successful **congregations** are shaped by faithful men, women and children, not by those with money who try to use wealth for forgiveness in pretending to be a man or woman of the cross. God would despise this and I would hope that most of us believe this to be a very very true statement. My thoughts and commentary along with the Words of God, Christ and the Holy Spirit throughout this book are intended to be helpful for elders, deacons, ministers and all other faithful servants who must cooperate together in harmonizing their places of worship. The energy and enthusiasm created by unity is contagious, leading to religiously hard workers for the Lord that are excited about the future of not only their **congregation**, but of surrounding **congregations**.

Whether it's a **congregation** of 5 or 525 that's looking to improve their record of success, you must work carefully with them and do them a favor when they realize you know what's taking place. Speak up! Not only is this a good idea, it's good to work with those who will help move the right people to the right place with the correct tools to do the job.

So much more could be said, but time is slipping from the reigns of our hands to His. Heaven awaits us! Always praise the Trio that make a great difference in our lives. Hope would not exist without God Himself, Christ Our Savior and the Powerful Holy Spirit. Don't ever lose sight of these Power Giants and the active Spirit they are. They provide steps for action to those on their way to Heaven and Eternity. Praise God for His actions and the kindness He has given us!

Life as we've grown to know it in yesteryear now gives to the obedient sons and daughters of God throughout The Great By And By. No doubt that God Almighty has demanded the best of Christ and The Holy Spirit to help mankind make safe and sure lives that will be welcomed in Heaven's abode.

We must gain the attention of our Christian Brothers and Sisters who have the Love of Christ and God, asking them for works that include applying attention toward teaching the Blessed Word of the Father of all Mankind! God teaches and many have learned, now understanding graciousness and the love that mothers and fathers have for their children, parents and loved ones.

Beloved Father God in Heaven. Thank you for your presence! Oh God, may You be pleased with this work that will be read by many who know that I am or will soon be with You in Paradise. I believe it was an honorable thing to do in the time I have remaining here on earth.

My wife, Mary Rose Harrell and I send a Sweet Goodbye to you and the same to our three children, John, Kelli and Jill, along with our kinfolk. Thanks to all who I've mentioned and I would have mentioned more if time permitted. And to those who raised us, we love you dearly. My parents, Dorothy and Reagan Harrell, as well as my wife's mother and father, Johnnie and Jess Rose.

Chapter Seventeen

The Final Chapter Presented to The World by Brother Dennis Moore

I conclude with an adventure into a very completed document, beautifully written by my very good Christian friend, Brother Dennis Moore, an elder of the Body of Christ that meets at the Congregation of Christ in Ruidoso, New Mexico. Brother Moore is a distinguished teacher of the Word who vigorously writes about what he has learned and what he believes. He is a gentleman of wisdom, recently turning 88 years of age. I must hasten to say that he is a gentleman of great courage and knows what the Lord has said. He is one that is full of many years of believing what he reads in the scriptures and is continuously searching for the truth, the whole truth, and nothing but the truth. I see him as a Great Man of God Almighty!

Introduction: The One Full of Grace and Truth (John 1:14)

1. **Has there ever been** any system of belief, ideology, religion, philosophy or human thought that has blessed mankind in a greater way than has the Christian Faith? **Is there** any religion that offers more hope or better explains the mysteries surrounding our existence than that offered in the biblical materials? **Any Religion,** worldview, or philosophical system must pass the most crucial test. Can it make sense of the human Predicament? Is it consistent with common sense? Does it answer the questions of the ages? Is it in the realm of plausibility or just wishful thinking? When put on the scales of History along with all the accumulated knowledge of the ages, plus our personal experiences, the truth that most appeals to our hearts and minds is that which provides Grace and understanding.

2. **The heart** of the message of "good news" announced by Christ provides what man desperately needs: **Grace and Truth. These gifts** are brilliantly presented in the first 14 verses of John's Gospel. These verses stand as the most profound prologue in the history of literature. **John** was a fisherman, unschooled and ordinary **(Acts 4:13). How could** he conceive such sublime truths about God and probe the deepest depths of theology? Nowhere do we better see the power of God's Spirit guiding the pen of the Apostle... a work of genius.

3. **"In the Beginning"** are the opening words of Genesis, with John using this expression to introduce a new creation through Jesus Christ--in the same category as the sublime importance of the physical creation itself. A bolder beginning cannot be imagined.

John, (The Biblical John) introduces us to the mystery of the eternal **WORD,** a term familiar to both Greeks and Jews. **By our words** we become known to others. **A person's** word is their character in expression. **Christ becomes** the medium to utter the mind, the nature, the thoughts, and the purpose of God. **The Word possesses** all the attributes of God but is distinct from God the Father; **existing** before creation and then becoming a part of creation; **in fellowship** with the father but leaving that fellowship to dwell among us, with the stunning climax that this "Word" which was God became flesh and dwelled among us! **There is** no other title that more clearly identifies Jesus Christ as God, with God revealing God to mankind. **This was** the term which made easier the transition from Jewish monotheism to Christian trinitarianism.

4.   **No one has ever seen God...has made Him known**. The Greek verb is "exegesato" **from which is derived our word**, "exegesis," **from which is also where "exit" comes from. It means** to "explain" or "interpret," to draw out, to move to darkness. **The Word** reveals the being and nature of God, which could only be presented by the incarnation. **It is from** the incarnation that we are to take our idea and understanding of God! Our first thought of God must forever be that which the incarnation so fully revealed! **God's Power** and Glory in creation does not reveal nor know Me. **(Jer. 24:7) But What Does God** want us to Know about Him? **(Jer. 9:23)** God provides the answer: that He understands and knows Me, that I am the Lord who exercises **Kindness** and **Justice**... For It, Glory; the **Word** declared **God's Love,** His Nature, His will, His Purpose. God's revelation to mankind moves from the abstract to the personal, from distance holiness to the nearness of a Father in Heaven; from a system of Law to one of Grace.

5.   **In Greek thought** the Word (Logos) meant to speak; a message of words; It had meaning for both the Greeks and the Jews. **Just as our** words reveal to others our hearts and minds, so Jesus Christ is God's **"Word"** to reveal His heart and Mind to us. A word is made of letters, and Jesus Christ is "Alpha and Omega" **(Revelation1:11),** the first and last letters of the Greek alphabet. Jesus Christ is God's last word to mankind, for He is the Climax of divine revelation. **(Heb.1:1)** John uses this term to describe Christ four times; twice in His Gospel; one in His first letter **(l John l:1);** and one in Revelation, **(Rev. 19:13).**

6.   **John speaks of seven Mysteries about the words**.

(1) **The Word is eternal**. "In the beginning was the word..." **The "Word" is** the source of all that is visible and existed before the totality of the material world.

(2) **The Word is distinct** from the Father. A different entry... "and the word was with

God..." Two distinct personalities in an internal relationship co- equal in divine attributes in the fullest sense of the concept. (Col. 2)

(3) "The Word was God" Jehovah's Witnesses translate this clause, "The Word was a God..." Polytheism; others have translated it. The Word was: Ambiguousness and misleading.

(4) The Word created...Through Him all things were made...The word "made" is an action that refers to an event rather than a process. **The universe** was not an action of cosmic coincidences; its origin came from the creative power and mind of God, not some evolution process through eons of time. Once you eliminate the impossible, whatever remains, no matter how improbable, must be the truth.

(5) The Word is the source of life... "In Him was life..." inherent life, the power to give life, restore life and extend life. Biological life is separated from inanimate creation.

(6) The Word is the provider of life. Man's understanding, his awareness, God's purpose and power are made available to mankind as He now brings new light into a world of darkness. Jesus Christ is God's sword to reveal God's heart and mind to us. **(John 14:9) There is** a parallel "in the beginning, God said, let there be Light." The **contrast** is between the old creation and a new creation; both come from the Word. **(Psalms 33:9) The first word** is **"Light,"** physical light for the world; the second announcement is spiritual light for all mankind. In Him was life and that life was the light of men. The true light that gives light to every man was coming to the world. **"The people walking in darkness have seen a great light." (Isa. 9:2) Grace was in the Old Testament, but it was like a candle compared with the brightness of the incarnation.**

(7) "The Word became flesh"

7.   **This is the stunning** climax of the Prologue. **This Word** transformed himself into a fleshly body. **The mind** of God becomes a person. The **Spirit** of God takes the form of a human body! God, Himself, was moving into the neighborhood! **The invisible God** has materialized into a human being. Man's longing to see God was done!

(1) God assumes a visible form. Believing in Christ is believing in God; looking at Christ is seeing God; **hearing** the words of Christ is listening to the words of God. **(John 12:44-49)** The invisible Spirit of God materializes in the face and body of Jesus. **Jesus was the** only person in history to plan His own birth--exchanging His perfect heavenly body for a frail body of blood, flesh and nerves. **The One** who brought the world into existence now brings Himself into our existence by being born as a human being...a staggering thought! **The Source** of all life reduces Himself to the weaknesses and limitations of human life and subjects himself to death! **He came** with the credentials of God but set aside the power by emptying himself.

(2) By the miracle of the virgin Birth. **(Isa 7:14; Matt. 1:18-25) Since Jesus** had no beginning; His very birth must explain how He could be born and yet not have a beginning. So we have the virgin birth because God, in His infinite power, can initiate life without sexual union. **This birth** insinuates Christ's pre-existence. **There is** a difference between the inherent power of creation and the bestowed power of procreation. **The infinite came** down to earth in the form of an infant! **The birth** was biological, the conception was supernatural; a life began, but it was not the beginning of the person represented by that life. **No other religion** -- Judaism, Hinduism, Buddhism or Islam--offers this astonishing contribution of an all-powerful God who willingly takes on the limitations, sufferings and identity of His creation.

(3) How does God want us to remember and react to this one-time event of such massive importance? **God's visit** to our planet is not remembered for dazzling displays of power, but primarily to bring the light of hope by grace, truth and representative suffering. **There was** no celestial rescue party to deliver Him from horrific evil. **His agony** was not mitigated by any superhuman anesthetic. **This was** the most astonishing act of condescension and self-humbling in recorded history. Here we have not just the fact of incarnation, but its meaning--it was not just a marvel of nature, but rather colossal in nature.

(4) How should we remember this Event?

> **a. We now know God as never before.** The one and only has made Him known.

> **b. We now know the truth (John 18:37)** that gives hope.

> **c. We now understand** that we now understood. **(Heb. 4:15)**

> **d. We now know the incarnation was not just a marvel of nature, it was a wonder of Grace. Paul writes (2ⁿᵈ Cor. 8:9) "You know the Grace of our Lord Jesus Christ, that though He was..."**

Full of Grace and Truth (John 1:14, 16-17)

1. **The incarnation** was the full manifestation, Grace and Truth because it was the greatest possible expression of God's compassion for people and the most perfect way of conveying that truth to our understanding. **Grace becomes the Most Important** word in the Bible because it captures the meaning of how God now relates to mankind, just as faith encompasses how we relate to God. **God's Grace is** His willingness to treat us as if we deserved to be heirs of His great inheritance. It is an **undeserved** favor, it is **forgiving love, it is unmerited kindness, it is a willingness to tolerate** the intolerable, to accept rather than exclude, to overlook instead of condemn; it is that precious gift offered by God which we can receive by the hand of faith.

2.   **The Word Grace is what makes the message about Jesus Christ** "Good News." The Word Truth is what makes it the most important message in the World! **Grace and Truth** have come into the World with Jesus Christ expressing the fullness of both. This verse is an affirmation that Jesus Christ is the basis on which we can know that God is good, gracious, and loving, and that this creation has meaning, and your life has purpose and value. The event of Christ was the time when God displayed His grace to mankind! It was the Year of God's favor **(Luke 4:18-19). The two** most desperately needed blessings in a confused and fallen world are introduced. This King would bring Grace and Truth to change our hearts, not domination and power to control our lives. **The Mission** of the Body of Christ is to dispense grace and truth. It is really the only thing the Body of Christ can offer to others because it is the pillar that supports the truth that God's grace has appeared to the entire world in the person of Jesus.

Without Grace We Have Law - Grace Stands in Contrast to Law

For the law was given by Moses, "grace and truth came through Jesus Christ" (John 1:17) Under Law, righteousness comes through from perfect obedience; under grace, God gives the gift of righteousness to **people in Christ.** This makes The Christian Faith unique among all believers in the world.

The Buddhists-The Hindus-Judaism-The Roman Catholic-Islam-Christian Faith- Legalism-Focus on Jesus-Without Grace-Performance

The Buddhists have an eight-fold path of right behaviors in order to reach their spiritual goal, which of all things is oblivion (Nirvana means the act of extinguishing yourself...absorbed...)

The Hindus' doctrine of Karma is complicated. **It has to do** with the punishment required to balance out his wrongs committed in previous lives. **The punishment** consists in reincarnations because there is no forgiveness in Hinduism. **You have** to work it out by being recycled until your debt is paid...

Judaism organized God's Laws (10 commandments) into 613 rules...later expanded into 1,512 for more correction. *To avoid defiling the Sabbath Day,* they outlawed 39 activities that might be construed as "work."

The Roman Catholic church has a Code of Canon law that contains 2,414 rules! Every mass is a symbolic sacrifice to expunge and expiate any violation or any rule.

Islam has its five pillars of practice which must be observed by the faithful if they are to enter Paradise. **Surprisingly**, none of the five address the value of another person's life... devoid of grace!

The Christian faith is the only religious faith that dares to make God's Love unconditional, free, no strings attached! **"For it is by Grace that you are saved through Faith...It is the gift of God." (Eph. 2:8) All we** can do is respond to God's Love and Grace by repentance, obedience and gratitude.

Legalism is the belief that one can be righteous by following law and commands perfectly. **It is an attempt** to be blameless by law rather than forgiven by grace. Such teaching nullifies the Grace of God and makes futile, the sacrifice of Christ.

The focus of Jesus' parables of Grace teach us about a God who takes the initiative toward us; **a grieving father** who runs to meet his wayward son, **a king** who cancels a debt too large for any servant to pay, **an employer** who pays one-hour workers the same as 12-hour workers, **a banquet-giver** who goes out to the ghettos and slums in search of undeserving guests.

Without Grace We Must Rely On Performance

We live in a Performance driven world. In nearly every human relationship, we have to earn our way. But in a family, only one thing Matters: Birth! The I.Q., skills, beauty, talent or accomplishments do not matter. True family love comes without conditions. Dennis Moore repeats: True family love comes without conditions. My three daughters did not have to earn approval and love, they had it from birth. The child with a birth defect or unattractive, or one with low performance on tests, or no outstanding skills! These kids merit the same love and affection.

Important Details - The Best Read:

One That Really Counts From The Book of Romans - Chapter Eight

Victory In Christ! Other Great Actions!

1. God Has Given Man Sovereignty, with which *He does* not interfere. He does not stop the **hand** that would strike another; the **tongue** that would curse another; the hate that would kill another; the **cruelty** that would rape another. God chose free-will instead of robots, machines or puppets. **We are** not animals guided only by instinct, but image-bearers guided by intellect. **(Job 38:36) We bear the image** of the Almighty--and with that exalted distinction, we can be **led by God's Spirit** and reflect divinity in our behavior, or we can yield to the weaknesses of our sinful nature and follow a path of demonic behavior. **We can** follow our intellect, our conscience--that noble desire to do what's right or we can yield to the impulse of our sinful desires: selfishness, greed, lust and hate! **We are guided** and influenced by a moral sensitivity to know what is right and what is wrong, with the impulse to do what is right, but with weaknesses that result in failure. **This never-ending** struggle is a part of our human situation and explains human behavior. **We are** a fallen species with a remnant of God's image within us and God's love **surrounding** us, and He has provided a plan of restoration for us. **In the Roman letter, Paul reveals** this glorious plan with its dominant feature of **grace**, making it possible for all people to be victorious in this titanic struggle with our flawed nature and with the outrageous fortunes that will come in life, and even the promise of surviving our inevitable destiny of death!

2. **There is no chapter** in the Bible as reassuring or consoling to the Christian as this, with its compelling arguments, its lofty eloquence and its concrete assurance of victory! **The follower of Christ** is given every possible security for his safety, well-being and ultimate victory! **We have** the unfailing **love of God**, the redeeming **work of Christ,** the presence and power of **the Holy Spirit,** and the assurance that even the good and bad **of all events** that can work together to secure the growth, welfare and salvation of God's people! One reason these 39 verses are so esteemed is because they begin with "no condemnation in Christ" and end with "no separation is possible from the love of God" and in between there is "no defeat in life for one in Christ regardless of what comes." **We have been given** a gift nothing can compare with and which nothing in all creation can take away or destroy. **We should** never be discouraged by life's adversities if we understand that they will come, and they can be a part of God's plan to actually serve to strengthen us. Our victory is not tenuous; just barely surviving. It **is never** in question, it is never in doubt, it is not by a slim margin or barely overcoming...rather with **boldness. Paul says, "We are**

more than Conquerors...more than conquerors, thru Jesus Christ!" He gives Victory and more victory! We need not fear life or death, things present or things to come, because Jesus Christ has provided and secured a triumphant victory for those believing. Yes, we will lose some battles--our sinful nature will sometimes win out, trouble and hardship will be a part of our journey, confusion will question our faith and pain may invade our bodies, loss may crush our heart--but ultimately, we will be triumphant, we will be victorious because we belong to the King of Kings and the Lord of Lords; and all the forces of Hell will not overcome His power--even the "gates of Hades will not prevail..." Death itself, will not impede the victory march.

The Presence of God's Spirit Prevents Death

1.   There should be no concern or excuse for a believer to ever be defeated by whatever this life brings! **To follow God's Spirit results in v6 "life and peace." To possess the Spirit of Christ is to be in a state of v10 "righteousness." v11 The Spirit will give life to our mortal bodies. v13 The Spirit of life empowers us! v14 The Spirit of God leads us! v15 The Spirit of God makes us sons of "God, not slaves of fear." v16 The Spirit of God "testifies" to our Spirit, giving us assurance of our Status: "sons of God, not slaves of fear"! v26 The Spirit helps us in our weakness. Our weakness is inhabiting fleshly bodies where sin is a permanent resident, and selfishness is a dominate motivator. He intercedes for us in our prayer; and on our behalf, "according to God's will."** (Not every prayer answered...)

2.   **What is meant** by God's Spirit? It is that part of God's image within each one of us. **When we are** led by that part of our nature, we have control of ourselves **instead** of being controlled by our sinful nature or sin "reigning" in our lives; it is subdued and subordinated to the weakness of the flesh, not the willfulness in our heart. **It means** striving to live your life by God's will as revealed in scriptures, as prompted by conscience, as exemplified by Christ. It means changing bad behavior by repentance. **It means** the subtle power of His presence is within us, helping us to overcome. **The Spirit** helps us in our weaknesses by prompting the motivation to so live, that willful, habitual, premeditated, deliberate acts of evil, never enter our mind or our life. **"Greater is He that is in you than he that is in the world." (1st John 4:4)**

A Glorious Future (Romans 8:18-27)

1.   There should be no apprehension about the Future! **v18** Our present sufferings will amount to nothing when placed next to the brilliance and Glory to be revealed! **Nothing**

150

in our present sufferings can compare to our future glory. **v19** Paul uses personification, (ascribing personhood to an inanimate object for better understanding). **v20 Paul tells that** all creation was subjected to frustration **v21** and to the bondage of decay. **v22 As one about** to give birth, nature has been groaning to (grieve, to sigh) with pain, **v23** eagerly awaiting deliverance. **When God** finished His creation; He pronounced it "good." **Today**, it is not good; it is a "groaning creation" suffering a sense of futility and uselessness and experiencing the bondage of decay. The **fall** of man had universal and catastrophic consequences. **The ground** was cursed (not man). Pain, suffering and death were introduced. **Man's fall** rippled like shockwaves throughout the universe! **All of nature** is personified both animate and inanimate.

v20 "Creation was subjected to frustration..." The **Greek** word means futility, without purpose. **Can we see** this today in windstorms, mud slides, tornadoes, floods, fires, volcanic eruptions, tsunamis, earthquakes, and devastation? **Why has** nature appeared to be so angry, intense, destructive throughout history and we have extreme events today? **We live** in a groaning, sighing, sobbing, suffering world. **All creation was** involved in man's fall and it will also be involved in man's redemption and "waits in eager expectation" for it! A curse was put on physical creation when man fell, and that curse will be removed, **(Rev. 21)** and all creation will participate in a complete makeover. **(Rev. 22:3)** "No longer will there be any curse."

2.   Science has unlocked the four laws of thermodynamics, (the laws of heat power). **Together** they form the foundation of modern science. **Surprisingly,** the second law is mentioned here by Paul: **(Rom. 8:21)** "Creation will be liberated from its bondage to decay." The universe is constantly losing energy and never gaining. It is like a wound-up clock gradually running down. Energy is being dissipated; stars run out of fuel. The sun will burn out in about a billion years. **Your coffee** gets cold; a perpetual motion device will always lose energy and run down. **While the quantity** of matter and energy remains the same (first law); the quality of matter and energy deteriorates gradually over time. Thus, usable energy is lost in the form of unusable energy. **The implications** of this law are astounding! **The universe** is not eternal, it had a beginning! It is losing energy and never gaining, eventually reaching the state known as absolute zero, estimated to be -459.67 Fahrenheit, which if reached, all molecular motion would stop! **That would** mean a long, cold, lifeless eternal night of nothingness! When God brought order out of chaos, He said: "**...let there be light.**" This explosion of energy and light filled the universe with life-giving energy and matter. This order will prevail as long as the earth endures, and God holds everything together! **Col. 1:17 "He is before all things and in Him all things hold together."**

3.	**(Rom. 8:23) We also groan inwardly** as we wait eagerly. We are already Children of God, so Paul is referring to the full realization of our inheritance in Christ...The redemption of our bodies. **The resurrection** is the **final** stage of our adoption. **(Rom. 8:29)/(Eph. 1:4)** The first stage was God's pre-determined purpose to adopt us as His children, those conforming to the image of His son. **This is** accomplished by faith in Him! **(Rom. 8:14) The second** is our present inclusion as children of God. **The Christian's** possession of the Holy Spirit is not only evidence of his present salvation, but also a pledge of his future inheritance.

Assurance of Victory (Rom. 8:28-39)

Paul encourages his readers to not doubt the power or the promises of God, reinforcing them with three affirmations:

(1) v28 God's Work ultimately accomplishes good for those who love Him. In "all things," **God assures** us that the difficulties of life are working for us and not against us. **The things** themselves may not be good; adversity, affliction, suffering, discipline, etc. In **(2ⁿᵈ Cor. 4:17)**, Paul reminds us: **"For our light and momentary troubles…"**

(2) God's purpose for man was pre-determined **(Eph. 1:4) "before the creation of the World," v29** for him to be conformed to the likeness of His Son. God determined beforehand that those who had faith in Christ would take on his identity and be part of a new race of humanity, purified from sin and prepared to live eternally in His presence. **All creation** moves within the purpose of God. **(Matt. 6:10)** That **purpose** is man's redemption for those who want it. **Thus, Christ** is referred to as the "First-born" (the highest position) among many brothers. **He is called** the "Last Adam" because he is the beginning and representative of the new creation.

(3) God's will for man is captured by four sovereign acts of God that encompass the whole of divine history:

1.	**Predestined (pre-determining) that our union with Christ by faith will restore man to his former state of glory and honor.**

2.	**Called (those who respond to the message), the call given by the gospel. (2ⁿᵈ Thes. 2:14)**

3.	**Justified (declared innocent or righteous) by their response stage.**

4.	**Glorified: all who will receive the promises contained in the message.**

This final stage is so firmly grounded in God's purpose that it is spoken of as if it had already happened.

These are the golden links in God's wondrous plan for His creation. God Predestined that faith in Christ would bring a declaration of righteousness and union with Christ to those responding. This appeal and call would come by the message of good news, and the response would result in being justified in God's eyes, and ultimately glorified in God's Kingdom. God's plan for man's salvation reaches from eternity past to eternity future. **Recognizing this, Paul asked five questions to guarantee the believer's security:**

(1) **v31** "What then, shall we say in response to this?"

(2) **v31** "If God is for us who can be against us?"

(3) **v33** "Who will bring any charge against those that God has chosen?"

(4) **v34** "Who is He that condemns? Any accusations will be thrown out of court because it is from God who justifies."

(5) **v35** "Who shall separate us from the love of Christ?" Meaning, His love for us, not ours for Him. **The apostle** asks if even bad life experiences could threaten our faith or our love: could trouble, hardship, persecution, famine, nakedness, danger, or sword? **Paul's answer** is a resounding "No," we are more than conquerors because our King has been victorious. **Paul points to the extremes of life** to give emphasis to his conviction: **He was** convinced that "neither death nor life, (extremes of the biological world) neither angels nor demons, (extremes of created spiritual armies) neither the present nor the future, (extremes in time) nor any powers, neither height nor depth (extremes in space) nor anything else in all creation, will be able to separate us from the love of god that is in Christ Jesus our Lord." **He left** nothing out, and God leaves no one out. **We can overcome** and be victorious in life because even with minds that can **punish us with guilt, there is no condemnation in Christ. Even though** we live in bodies infested with a sinful nature, the presence of God's Spirit can "put to death its misdeeds." **Even though** we have lost so many battles in our life, there is nothing that can ultimately defeat us.

The Apostle John sees a vision recorded in **(Rev. 19)** of the "curtain of heaven standing open" and **revealing the scene of a rider on a white horse, called Faithful and True:**

"He had eyes **blazing like fire, crowns** were upon His head, He was dressed in a robe dipped in blood; out of His mouth came a **sharp sword**. **The armies** of heaven were following him, and they, also, were riding on white horses, dressed in fine linen, white and clean. **His name is the Word of God. His title** was written on the robe and thigh: **King of Kings and Lord of Lords**." **It is the march of triumph! No enemy** can stand before the penetrating blaze of his eyes or the razor-sharp sword coming from his mouth. He alone is King of Kings and Lord of all. **Those following** this victorious King on their white horses are the redeemed, of all ages, dressed in garments of purity, having overcome all enemies; they share in the victory of their King! The vision of **(Rev. 7:14)** coincides: **"These are they who have come out of the great tribulation (persecution) and have washed their robes and made them white in the blood of the Lamb."** Hallelujahs erupt from a sea of angels, a chorus of praise filling the universe! They have overcome! Thanks be to God! He gives us the victory through our Lord Jesus Christ. **(1st John 5:4) "This is the victory that has overcome the world, even our faith."**

Love to All,

Dennis Moore

My good friends and neighbors, this concludes the efforts of Brother Dennis Moore to spread the Word of God to endless boundaries of people around the world. Dennis is a phenomenal writer. As you can tell, the last chapter is a winner. Thank You and God Bless you! My personal thanks for Brother Moore's great contribution! You should have received great Joy from reading these last pages! This will be my last thank you for kindness and keeping the faith! Continue to love and honor God with best intentions! How sweet it will be in Heaven when we all get together in such a splendid place. I can hardly wait to see Him, listen to Him and Love Him!

God Be With You!
Happy Days To Each of You!
May He Bless You and Keep you!
Roger

Salute to Brother & Sister Moore

A Salute to Brother Dennis Moore and wife Jackie for all their work and acceptance and love of all people! This is a special tribute for both!

I hereby salute this great Father and Mother for all they do for people, for all whom they have met and cared for, and have shown the love and kindness of Christ!

Dennis and Jackie Moore have worked tirelessly for many years in providing so much for others. They live the kind of lives that bring love and care to so many people, many who have come and gone and many who have already left this earth to be with God.

We take the time to bow our heads and offer our hearts to those who may be in great need. In His name, we show gratitude and pray for continued assistance in bringing other people to serve in the unselfish manner that both Dennis and Jackie have, to work for the Lord and live an honorable life. Amen.

Love to the two of you,

Dr. Roger Harrell

Taking The Side Of Jesus

Whose Side Are You On?

Understand this! God, His Son Jesus and The Holy Spirit want powerful relationships with people who love one another and become members of His Ekklesia (**Assembly** or **Congregation**) upon believing and being baptized for the remission of sin, being fully immersed within the waters of baptism and acknowledging that Jesus was the living Son of God who accepted our punishment by dying a horrible death upon the cross to take our sins away through His crucifixion.

I love my God so much and when I hear what He says, I follow Him in whatever way He desires, always joyful in proclaiming His name! Thank you for your kind attention. God speaks and I listen. If it is in the Bible and truly understood, it is for you, me and everyone.

Thank God for everything that He has so generously given to us! May you and I continue our work for the Kingdom!

In His name we pray, Amen!

Roger, Mary, John, Kelli, Jill and Families!

www.ingramcontent.com/pod-product-compliance
Lightning Source LLC
Chambersburg PA
CBHW081511040426
42447CB00013B/3190